To Rob

January 26, 2022

Nannybones Kitchen

Blessings

Nancy Greenspan

First Printing, 2021

Printed in the United States by Moeller Printing-Indianapolis, IN.

Nancy Grandquist products, books, sermons, videos & CD's can be found at NancyGrandquist.com.

Find Nancy on Spotify & iTunes.

For bookings, please visit NancyGrandquist.com.

Watch on YouTube at Grandquist Ministries.

ISBN 978-0-578-99607-3

Nannybones Kitchen

By Nancy Grandquist

Dedication

This book is dedicated to you my family and
friends. For every time you cook a meal, and
pour out on others, that you will know the
deepest satisfaction, the sweetest reward of
gratitude and love from those you serve.

"May the food we eat
and the drink we drink
satisfy, bring long life,
joy, and strength."

NG

Contents

Forward

Dear Reader,

I hope this little book takes you on a voyage of discovery and making memories and new culinary creations with family, friends close enough to be family, and perhaps even an enemy or two. Before we dive in, I'd like to give you a peek into the cadence of my heartbeat: my family, my world, cooking fabulous food, and loving Jesus.

Some of the best times of my life have been spent in the kitchen—not just my kitchen, but my mother's, grandmother's and grownup children's kitchens, the kitchens of close and dear friends, and kitchens everywhere. I cannot describe the happiness I experience sharing the designated space of a stove, a counter, a sink, with people I love. I am overcome with joy unspeakable and howling laughter when I recall memories from some wrecked and ruined recipes that came out of my oven looking more like a burnt sacrifice than Sunday dinner.

(Speaking of burnt sacrifices, I've included a special story about my mother's baked girdle. It is hilarious.)

I was mostly a rambunctious child and definitely nocturnal by nature. I usually came alive a few minutes before the closing of the day. I am humbly grateful for my sweet mom who patiently put up with my midnight madness of starting a baking project or cooking up some extraordinary concoction that most certainly was destined for our dog, Blitzie, who willingly ate my blunders. But if she didn't—or couldn't—it would go to the chickens. They ate everything.

The love of cooking and baking has changed the destiny of many and altered the course of impossibly difficult situations.

I recall the story in I Samuel 25 of a man named Nabal, which in Hebrew meant "fool". His name described him perfectly, for he most assuredly had lost sight of his senses. He was a harsh, arrogant, stubborn man who defied David's army. Inexcusably rude, he commanded his soldiers to gather up all the men in David's army, then commenced to humiliate them by cutting off their armor so that their hinder parts were exposed. Then, adding insult to injury, he had his soldiers cut off the men's beards.

He had no idea who he came against. David was incensed when he heard what Nabal had done. He called 400 of his best warriors and set out to finish off Nabal and his men. (My goodness, this is turning out to be a vicious, violent, bloodletting story for a recipe book. Stay with me. We are almost to the good part.)

Abigail (I love that name) heard about her poor, doomed husband's actions. She never told Nabal her strategy. She just gathered a feast of everything delicious, loaded up her donkey transport team and headed out to find David and his army. What a brave, courageous woman, with just the right touch of audacity. When Abigail saw David, she bowed before him and talked him out of his plan for Nabal and his boys. Whew. What a food and feast treaty that brilliant, wise lady put together. Abigail and her faithful, furry donkeys came in like the Marines to save the day. When Nabal heard how his wife had saved him and his men, it was lights out for him and he died a few days later. Guess who got the girl? Yep! When David heard that Abigail was a free woman, he immediately proposed and they lived happily ever after. The End.

But, it is not the end for us. We have the power to change the course of our lives and even intervene and help others find a way to resolve their conflicts. We can bring restoration to a troubled family relationship, a marriage, a failing business venture, and even to appease a church board. I have witnessed the wonderful, miracle-working power of prayer and taking a hot apple pie out of the oven, serving up a slice of it with warm vanilla sauce and a scoop of ice cream, and watching the face of a soured, grumpypants grouch-pot turn into a teddy bear.

I remember reading the sweetest statement years ago that if we really wanted world peace, everyone should be required to have an afternoon snack of graham crackers with chocolate frosting (my favorite), a glass of milk and a nap. This testifies to the gentle, extraordinary influence that we have emanating straight out of the pots, pans, and bowls in our kitchens, into the mouths of babes and menfolk. (I could put women in there too, but mostly we are the queens of culinary delights. By the time we get it all tasted, cooked, served, cleaned and swept, we are ready for bed. It's just what we do.)

We save the nations with our spatulas, spoons and stoves. Our weapons are banana cakes with buckets of cream cheese frosting, yeast rolls dripping with butter, fried chicken with mashed potatoes and killer gravy. There is no wall or fortress we cannot penetrate. The battle is the Lord's, and we win!

Pass the biscuits.
—Nan

INTRODUCTION

My earliest and fondest childhood memories involve food, whether that was Mom serving us Cap'n Crunch in the hot tub before school, or a more refined dish like shrimp piquant over a candlelight dinner. We helped Mom peel the shrimp with great expectation of our anticipated feast.

Food and sitting together at the table was more than a quick meal to be consumed. Mom has always made eating a time of connection, celebration, and communion. Her love language is serving us fabulous and savory dishes like her incredible Fried Chicken with Butter and Scallion Dipping Sauce, topped off with her famous Gravenstein Apple Pie.

This art of cooking has been passed down from her mother and her mother's mother, and I have found the same joy watching my children sitting around my table laughing, talking and enjoying my own cooking. These recipes that you are soon to discover and enjoy are simple, fabulous, and connected to thousands of our family memories. If you aren't lucky enough to sit at Nannybones' table in person, here's a chance to cook up some of her best dishes and celebrate with your own family!

So, as my Mom says at our holiday dinners together as we raise our Martinelli's apple cider, "To all our days!" Indeed, and may they be filled with moments made at the table surrounded by the ones we love.

Heidi Grandquist King

Substitutions

Baking Powder, 1 teaspoon	1/2 teaspoon cream of tartar + 1/2 teaspoon baking soda
Bread Crumbs, 1/4 cup	3/4 cup soft bread crumbs
Broth, 1 cup	1 teaspoon broth base or bouillon granules + 1 cup of hot water
Cornstarch, 1 tablespoon	2 tablespoons all purpose flour
Flour- Self Rising, 1 cup	1 cup all purpose flour + 1 1/2 teaspoon baking powder + 1/4 teaspoon kosher salt
Garlic, 1 clove	1/2 teaspoon bottled minced garlic paste or 1/8 teaspoon garlic powder
Lemon Juice, 1 tablespoon	1 1/2 teaspoon apple cider vinegar or white wine vinegar
Onion, chopped	1/2 cup green onion or 2 tablespoons dried minced onions
Sugar, Brown, 1 cup	1 cup granulated sugar + 2 tablespoons molasses
Sugar, 1 cup	1 cup brown sugar or 2 cups sifted powdered sugar
Wine, Red, 1 cup	1 cup broth for savory dishes

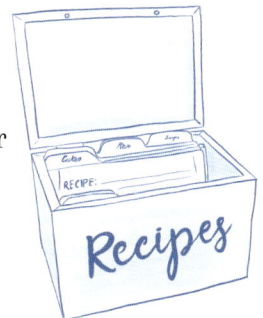

Recipes

Something Sweet

My life is uncertain, so I have dessert first.

"When I was really hurting, I prayed to the Lord. He answered my
prayer, and took my worries away."

Psalms 118:5

Fabulous Old Fashioned Fudge

-My Mother in Law's recipe

- 3 Cups sugar
- 1 1/2 Cups milk
- 1/4 Cup unsweetened Hershey's Cocoa
- 1/3 stick butter
- 1 tsp vanilla
- Note: add a touch of peanut butter for extra flavor

1. Put sugar, milk and cocoa in a pan. Stir and cook until boiling slows, test the mixture.
2. Have a glass of cold water near the stove. Drop a small amount of the fudge into the cold water, if it forms a soft ball, it is ready.
3. Take the pan off of the burner, then add butter and vanilla and nuts. Mom always added a tablespoon of peanut butter.
4. Pour into a buttered dish. After it cools, cut into pieces.

Note: If using a candy thermometer, fudge will be ready when thermometer reads between 235-240F.

My mom in law Thelma Venturella was an expert at this! After 50 years of trying to make her fabulous recipe and failing, yes for 50 years my fudge came out as hard as granite or only edible with a spoon or straw! I finally gave up and bought a candy thermometer. I am so proud to tell you I am finally making the perfect fudge!

Brilliant Banana Foster

- 6 Tbsp butter
- 1 Cup lightly packed brown sugar
- 1/2 tsp cinnamon
- 1/4 Cup banana liquor (optional)
- 4 firm bananas, peeled, halved lengthwise then crosswise
- 1/4 Cup amber rum
- Vanilla Ice Cream (Haagen-Daz or Bluebell)

1. In pan, melt butter, then add brown sugar and cinnamon. Stir.
2. When completely melted, add in bananas.
3. Coat bananas thoroughly and move to side of pan.
4. Pour in rum and light on fire!
5. Allow flame to extinguish.
6. Serve over ice cream or waffles. You can also try this recipe as a strawberry foster!

Heidi's Favorite Butter Cake

- 1 Box Yellow Cake Mix
- 4 eggs
- 1 stick butter
- 8 oz. package cream cheese
- 1 box powdered sugar

1. Preheat oven to 350 degrees.
2. Use a glass baking dish.
3. Mix by hand cake mix, 2 eggs and melted stick of butter.
4. Place in bottom of dish (grease glass dish, do not grease metal pan).
5. With an electric mixer, beat together cream cheese, 2 eggs and a box of powdered sugar till creamy.
6. Pour cream cheese mixture over cake mixture.
7. Bake at 350 degrees for 40 minutes or until golden brown or test with a toothpick (put toothpick into the middle of the cake, if it comes out clean it is done.)

Delicious & Delectable Date Bars

-Trucie Rooks shared this family recipe with me in 1979. It is insanely delicious!

- 1 1/2 Cups of oats
- 1 Cup of dark brown sugar
- 2 sticks of butter (melted)
- 1 1/2 Cups of flour
- 1 tsp soda (sift soda with flour)
- 1/4 tsp salt
- 1 package dates
- 1/3 Cup sugar
- 1/2 Cup milk
- 1 Tbsp butter

1. Preheat oven to 350 degrees.
2. In a bowl, mix together oats, dark brown sugar, flour and soda.
3. Spread half of the mix on the bottom of a pan, pressing down firmly. Set aside remaining mixture.
4. Put all remaining ingredients in a saucepan, cook over low heat.
5. Once it cooks down, spread over crumb mixture and use remaining crumb mixture to spread over the top of the date filling.
6. Gently press crumb mixture into place.
7. Bake at 350 till golden brown.
8. Cool before cutting into bars.

Pentecostal Peanut Brittle

- 3 Cups sugar
- 1 Cup Karo syrup
- 1/2 Cup water
- Heat to 250 degrees (use Candy thermometer)
- Add 1 1/2 Cups Raw peanuts
- 1/8 cube butter
- 2 tsp soda
- 1 1/2 tsp salt

1. Heat sugar, karo syrup, water, raw peanuts and cubed butter on medium in a saucepan.
2. Cook until peanuts pop. Candy will turn brownish color.
3. Take from heat and stir in soda and salt.
4. Beat to remove bubbles. Pour into buttered cookie sheet or buttered pie pans.
5. When pan cools, carefully turn upside down and remove from pan.

I think my mother and I have made enough Peanut Brittle to pave the road from San Francisco, California to Albuquerque, New Mexico...Many church buildings, projects, even orphanages have been built by the proceeds of the very spirit of Pentecostal Peanut Brittle.

Holiday Candy Balls

- 1 can Eagle Brand milk
- 2 boxes Confectioner's sugar
- 2 bags chopped Pecans
- 2 cans flakes Coconut
- 3/4 block paraffin wax
- 12 ounce bag Chocolate Chips

1. Mix together: milk, powdered sugar and add chopped pecans and coconut.
2. Paraffin wax and chocolate chips should be melted in a double broiler or a heavy pot.
3. Roll into small balls and drop into paraffin and melted chocolate chips.
4. Lift balls out with fork or tongs. Put on wax paper to dry.
5. Dip one ball at a time.

Divine Divinity

-By Jessie Green Alred

- 2 1/2 Cups sugar
- 1/2 Cup light corn syrup
- 1/2 Cup hot water
- 1/4 tsp salt
- 2 stiff-beaten egg whites
- 1 tsp vanilla
- 1/2 Cup Candied cherries

1. In a pan, combine sugar, corn syrup, water and salt. Cook to very hard-ball stage at 260 degrees.
2. Beat stiff-beaten egg whites.
3. Slowly pour corn syrup in a thin stream over beaten egg whites, beating continuously.
4. Beat till mixture holds it shape (about 4-5 minutes).
5. Stir in vanilla and cherries (leave out cherries if preferred).
6. Drop by heaping tablespoons onto waxed paper, lifting and twirling spoon to form a peak.
7. If divinity becomes to stiff for twirling, add a few drops of hot water.

I left home at a very young age and attended
a private Christian School.

Jess was my roommate. She was in college and I was in high school. She was 19 and I was 14 1/2.

She was a deep, steady, scholar of scripture, a spiritual guru. She was also a fiery preacher. I was a skinny kid trying to keep the seams straight in my nylons on my toothpick legs. She was my guardian angel, Jessie named her one and only child after me. Through-out the last 55 years Jessie has been a constant in my life. She has always loved and adored me and I have loved her the very same. Thank God for gifts like Jessie Green Allred. She is a rare treasure in this world.

Lilly

She was born in the old country. She was Assyrian and could put on a Persian feast exquisite enough for God, The Saved, and The Blessed (and whomever else might partake of the Marriage Supper of The Lamb)! Her name was Lilly.

She was the matriarch of her family and she capably managed several ranches of fine peaches and a few grape vineyards. Fondly, I conjure up pictures and conversations in my memories that fill my senses with joy and nostalgic sentimentality. Those were golden summer days. All of our children were small, so our entire visit was filled with the constant ebb and flow of laughter, screams of excitement or frustration, and the sounds of children squabbling and then later making up. I can still see the old father, Don, bent over a heap of coals and dried grapevines, nursing the fire that would barbeque the marinated lamb, tomatoes, onions and eggplants.

Lilly's rice was like none I had ever tasted. It was most definitely on this side of the Divine! Lilly's beautiful daughter with raven black hair, green eyes and creamy pale skin always made us feel so welcome. She would bake a coconut pie from scratch, and then would make homemade vanilla ice cream with her special fudge sauce.

I never really understood Lilly. Her clothes were mostly wrinkled with a few drips of this and a little of that splattered across the fabric in some haphazard pattern. Her hair was gathered into a loose bun, and there were always a few unruly, stray tendrils of hair that would creep out and surround her face. Often when we arrived for our visit, she would still be wearing her coat from either working in the fields or coming in from a Sunday church service. Her hands were rough with unkempt fingernails. She didn't care what we (or anyone else, for that matter) thought about her. She was a sturdy, no-nonsense girl/woman and she knew what and who she was.

Today I remembered Lilly. It was frigid outside after our Sunday service. I wore my old cashmere black coat with black leather patches on the elbows that covered the large holes. My hair was blowing everywhere, my bun was loose, and my house shoes were layered with mud. I had purchased several bags of fertilizer earlier in the fall and was just getting around to using those bags to fertilize my Gravenstein apple trees.

Thinking about that autumn day brings a stab of pain to my heart. That was the last time I shared a ride with my Dad. He was so fragile. He rode shotgun with me to the nursery where they sell mulch and other earthy-smelling products. I was having trouble tying down the tarp that day, so I used the bags of fertilizer to weigh the tarp down while Dad sat in the cab in the front of the truck.

Today, I wiped away tears with the back of my hand, leaving a streak of mud across my face. Then I pulled a bobby pin out of my hair and pierced the top of the bag. It opened, and I extravagantly poured out the vitamin mix. My dad would have loved it. He left us several years ago, and every day I run into this huge bank of memories. I see him and I tell him I love him and miss him. And then I smile, thinking of the disheveled picture that I must present.

I realized I am Lilly! Or at least I am some modified version of Lilly's "no-nonsense, let's get it done, 'if you don't like it lump it,' spirit," Awwww, yes!!!! At last! I finally get it!!! THIS is where the fun comes in - eccentric, eclectic, entirely better than ever before! My WORD, Lilly, how you must be smiling when you look down at me.

Nancy Leonard's Coconut Cream Pie

-Lilly's Girl

- 1/3 Cup cornstarch
- 2/3 Cup sugar
- 1/3 tsp salt
- 2 Cups scalded milk
- 3 egg yolks beaten well
- 2 Tbsp butter
- 1 tsp vanilla
- 1 Cup coconut

Meringue:
- 3 egg whites
- 1/4 tsp cream of tartar
- 1/4 tsp salt
- 1/2 tsp vanilla extract
- 6 Tbsp sugar

1. Preheat oven to 425-450 degrees.
2. Blend cornstarch, sugar and salt together, then add in beaten egg yolks.
3. Slowly stir in scalded milk. Cook in double boiler until mixture thickens.
4. Add to rest of mixture, stir and cook 2 minutes.
5. Remove from heat and cool 5 minutes.
6. Add butter, vanilla and 1/2 cup coconut.
7. Pour into cooked crust.
8. Prepare meringue.

Meringue:
1. Beat egg whites at high speed until foamy.
2. Adding in gradually the cream of tartar, salt and vanilla.
3. Continuing to beat, add by tablespoons the sugar, until mixture is stiff and forms peaks.
4. Spread on cool pie filling and bake at 350 degrees about 15 minutes or until brown on peaks.
5. Cool away from drafts.

Mom's Sour Cream Walnuts

- 1/2 Cup sour cream
- 2 Cups of sugar
- pinch of salt
- 1 tsp vanilla
- 5 to 6 Cups of walnuts

1. Cook ingredients on medium heat and add in walnuts.
2. Stir and pour out onto wax paper.

Grandma Thelma made holidays very special by making her famous sour cream walnuts! What made these extra delicious is that the walnuts were harvested from her own trees, 50 acres of them! What an amazing gift to be able to experience the freshest, organic taste of just picked walnuts from the family ranch!

There is nothing quite like enjoying the pure, pleasure of walnuts grown on family land. To this day I can hardly bring myself to buy a bag of walnuts in the grocery store. What a gift it was to visit mom and receive a bag of her beautiful walnuts, all carefully shelled by her own hand. Thank you sweet mom of my darling husband, you had vision and foresight to plant trees and keep planting!

Caramel Corn

-This is a showstopper!

- 1 Cup butter
- 2 Cups brown sugar
- 1/2 Cup karo syrup
- 1 tsp salt
- 8 quarts (32 cups) popped corn (Can use pre-popped corn and kettle corn flavor adds an extra punch to the finished product.)
- 1/2 tsp baking soda

1. Preheat oven to 250 degrees.
2. Pop the popcorn or use pre-popped corn. Place popped corn in a large roaster or disposable, lightly greased pan.
3. Cook the following ingredients on medium heat until it reaches 248 degrees: butter, brown sugar, karo syrup, salt.
4. When temperature is reached, add in 1/2 teaspoon of baking soda and mix well.
5. Pour over corn and mix thoroughly.
6. Bake at 250 degrees for 45 minutes, stirring every 15 minutes.
7. Place on waxed or parchment paper to cool.

Note: I store my caramel corn in a large jar with a lid.

Sometimes I do the Recipe at 1 1/2 times for the same amount of popcorn. It just gives a little more coating on each kernel. Caution! It's addicting!
Thank you Janet Brannon, I'm forever ruined after eating your caramel corn!

Lovely Lemon Bars

- 1 stick Butter
- 1/4 Cup Powered Sugar
- 1 Cup Flour
- 2 eggs
- 2 Tbsp lemon juice
- 1 Cup sugar
- 2 Tbsp flour
- 1/2 tsp baking powder

1. Preheat oven to 350 degrees.
2. Mix butter, powdered sugar and 1 cup flour in a bowl thoroughly and press in an 8x9 or 9x9 pan and bake for 15-20 minutes at 350 degrees.
3. While crust is baking, beat together eggs, lemon juice, sugar, 2 tablespoons of flour and 1/2 teaspoon baking powder.
4. Pour mixture over baked crust and bake 25 minutes at 350 degrees or until light brown.
5. Should be soft inside.
6. Sprinkle with powdered sugar and cut into bars.

Chocolate Marshmallow Crisps

- 1 Package 6 ounces Semi Sweet Morsels
- 1/4 Cup Peanut Butter
- 3 Cups Kellogg's Rice Krispics Cereal
- 1 Cup Miniature Marshmallows

1. Melt chocolate morsels and peanut butter together in large saucepan over very low heat, stirring constantly until smooth.
2. Remove from heat.
3. Stir in Rice Krispies and marshmallows.
4. Press mixture evenly into buttered 8x8x2 pan.
5. Chill until firm.
6. Cut into squares.

IRene's Chocolate pie

- 2 Cups milk
- 1 Cup sugar or Wheylow (sugar substitute)
- 3 Tbsp cornstarch (mix in with sugar)
- 1 Tbsp butter
- 1 brick of semi sweet chocolate. (Piece of the bar)

Flaky to a fault Pie Crust:

- 1 ½ Cups flour
- 1 tsp salt
- 2 Tbsp sugar
- ½ Cup oil
- 2 Tbsp milk

1. Preheat oven to 400 degrees
2. In a pot, combine all ingredients and cook on medium-low heat for 10-12 minutes until thickened.
3. Pour into prepared pie crust.

Pie Crust:

1. Mix all pie crust ingredients and press into pie pan.
2. Prick with a fork all over and bake at 400 degrees for 12-15 minutes.

My #BFF Suzi Toadvine and her Prince husband Rick took care of us after I had foot/toe surgery. Richard M. had fallen from his horse and fractured his wrist. We were a walking wreck with his arm and wrist in a cast and me with an artificial joint replacement in my big toe and a ton of stitches, I was mostly laying down, foot up for several weeks.
They cooked and cared for us and treated us like family. This was Irene's Recipe, Rick's mother, this chocolate pie tastes like it came from heaven. Ridiculously delish!

My Mother's White Cake

-With Strawberry Yogurt and Homemade Vanilla Frosting

- 1 box Betty Crocker super moist white cake mix
- 3/4 Cup of water
- 1/3 Cup of vegetable oil
- 3 egg whites
- 1 Container (6 oz) Yoplait Original Strawberry yogurt

1. Preheat oven to 350 degrees.
2. Put cake mix in a bowl and add ingredients.
3. Mix slow for 1 minute then mix on medium for 2 minutes until thoroughly mixed.
4. Pour batter into prepared pans.
5. Bake at 350 degrees for 25 minutes or until golden brown.

Frosting:

- 1/2 cube butter
- 3 Cups powdered sugar
- 1/4 Cup milk
- 1 tsp vanilla

Frosting:

1. In a bowl, melt butter in microwave.
2. Add powdered sugar and stir in milk.
3. Add vanilla.
4. Stir until a smooth consistency.
5. Frost cake only after it is cool.

Add On for a Magical Moment of Madness!

1. Wash and prepare fresh strawberries, blackberries and blueberries and put fruit in bowl.
2. Set aside 2 cups of strawberries (heavily sugar them, then purée until smooth)
3. Pour over remaining fruit.
4. Cover and let sit for at least an hour.
5. Right before you serve the cake pour the fruit mixture over frosted cake.

Pavlova

-Pavlova in a crock-pot from Ida Montano Foster & her friend Liz in Belfast, Ireland

- 6 egg whites
- 12 oz castor white sugar
- 2 tsp corn starch
- 1 tsp white vinegar
- 1 tsp vanilla

1. Beat egg whites and gradually add sugar, corn starch, vinegar and vanilla until stiff.
2. Turn crock pot on low.
3. Line crock pot with wax paper so you can lift pavlova out when cooked.
4. Pour mixture into pot, cover pot with clean tea towel and put lid on.
5. Cook on low for about 1 1/2 hours.
6. Leave until completely cold before taking out.
7. Decorate with whipped cream and fresh fruit.

Movie Star Rose's Famous Banana Cake

- 1 Box Betty Crocker Super Moist Yellow Cake Mix
- 1 Cup sugar
- 1 Cup self rising flour (you can make self rising flour yourself! Just add 1 1/2 tsp baking powder and 1/4 tsp salt to a cup of all purpose flour)
- 4 eggs
- 3/4 Cup oil
- 5 to 6 large bananas (ripe)
- Vanilla and rum up to 2 Tbsp
- 1 Cup pecans chopped

Frosting:
- 1 Cup soft butter
- 2 8 ounce cream cheese
- 8 Cups powdered sugar
- Add vanilla or rum or both... Can add vanilla and drink rum LOL

1. Preheat oven to 350 degrees.
2. Beat bananas and add oil, sugar and flour, then add eggs, cake mix and pecans.
3. Pour into prepared pan.
4. Bake at 350 degrees until golden brown.

Frosting:
1. Beat butter and cream cheese together.
2. Add powdered sugar and vanilla and rum if you like!
3. Frost the cake after it is cool and be generous with the frosting. Lavish it quite heavily on the cake!

Make sure you leave a little in the bowl for you and yours truly to have a spoonful on the side!

Get ready for the stampede! There will be no leftovers!

Movie Star Rose's Famous Banana Cake

Fried Pie Dough

-My blue eyed Sicilian BFF Janet's pie crust for her ridiculous fried pies.

- 2 1/2 Cups all purpose flour
- 1/4 tsp salt
- 2 1/2 Tbsp granulated white sugar for savory filling dough
- 3 1/2 Tbsp granulated white sugar for sweet filling dough
- 1/3 Cup cold vegetable shortening
- 2/3 Cup cold and cubed butter
- 1/3 to 2/3 Cup ice water

Note: This dough can be frozen in advance. Just place each wrapped dough in a separate freezer bag. I make several recipes in advance and keep a supply in the freezer use as needed.

Use canned fruit for sweet pies and meat filling for savory pies.

1. In a large mixing bowl, sift together the flour, salt and sugar (choose the sugar amount to the type of filling you will use, savory or sweet.
2. Add the very cold shortening and break it up, blend it in, with a pastry cutter to small pea size bits.
3. Add the cold butter cubes and work it into the flour with a pastry cutter. Work it quickly, so the butter doesn't get soft, mix until it is crumbly, similar to a very coarse cornmeal.
4. Add the ice water, a little at a time, until the mixture comes together forming a dough.
5. Blend together with a spatula or wooden spoon, Hands in the dough will melt the fats and make the dough tough.
6. Bring the dough together into a ball.
7. When it first comes together stop working it. Over worked dough is tough dough.
8. Divide the dough in half, create a ball, and flatten it to form about a 1 inch disk shape.
9. Wrap each disk in plastic wrap and chill in the refrigerator for about 20 to 40 minutes.
10. On a floured surface roll each disk out to make the shape and size of your desired use.

Our Family Treasure

My gram and my mom worked in the seasonal apple cannery. My brother David and I would occasionally get to go visit them on their lunch hour, we relished every moment of these adventures.

My gram worked sorting the good apples from the bad, discarding apples that were too bruised or rotten. My mother's job was to place the apples into a wickedly fast peeling device, one on the right and one on the left. I admired how coordinated and accurately she placed the apples. My gram worked hard and saved enough money to buy a small farm on Eddie Lane in Sebastopol, my mom paid off my piano and bought our school clothes. The quiet sacrifice of these two matriarchs of my life continue to fill my soul with awe and wonder.

I miss them so much.

They treated us to fresh Gravenstein Apple juice and apple slices and everything apple. The fragrance of a Gravenstein apple is intoxicating and puts my head in a spin remembering all the years we would peel apples and "put by". That was my Gram's word for canning. We made apple butter and stewed apples and all things apple. Now every August I try to drive to Sebastopol and get a couple of boxes of apples. These apples only run for 2 or 3 weeks so be intentional about getting them while you can. This past August was the first time I didn't have my mom beside me peeling apples. It was a strange reality, bittersweet for sure.

I have learned to cherish every memory and every moment shared by those I love. Life is Beautiful. Take time to smell the apples.

Gravenstein Apple Pie

- 10 to 15 Gravenstein apples
- 3 Cups sugar
- 1 tsp ground cloves
- 1 tsp ground nutmeg
- 1 1/2 Tbsp cinnamon
- 1/2 Cup flour

1. Preheat oven to 350-375 degrees.
2. Peel apples and cut into pieces.
3. Add all ingredients being sure to thoroughly coat apples in mixture.
4. Fold apples into pie crust.
5. Bake at 350-375 for one hour.

Serve Mom's vanilla sauce on page 172 over a warm piece of pie.

Pumpkin Crumb Cake

-This is so easy to make!

- One large can of pumpkin
- 12 ounce can evaporated milk
- 3 eggs
- 1 Cup sugar
- 1/2 tsp salt
- 1 1/2 tsp ginger
- 1 1/2 tsp cinnamon
- 1 tsp nutmeg
- 1 box yellow cake mix
- 1 stick butter

1. Preheat oven to 350 degrees.
2. Mix the first 8 ingredients thoroughly.
3. Grease a 9x13 inch pan and pour mixture into pan.
4. Sprinkle dry cake mix all over the top carefully.
5. Melt butter then drizzle over the top.
6. Carefully place the pan into the oven and bake at 350 degrees for 45-50 minutes.
7. Cool the pumpkin crumb cake before serving.
8. Put a lavish spoonful of whipping cream on top of each serving.

Pieces can be inverted with the pumpkin on top or with the crumbs on top. This is a delightful dessert!

Gravenstein
Apple Pie

Meredith's Mom's Ice Cream Cake

- 2 sleeves of Oreo cookies. (Plus extra Oreo's for crumbling on top)
- 1 stick of butter melted
- 1 carton Vanilla Ice Cream
- Mrs. Richardson Hot Fudge
- Cool Whip

1. Crush up Oreos in large ziplock bag and pour butter in on crushed Oreos, and mix well.
2. Press into 9x13 Pyrex dish.
3. Freeze for at least 1 hour.
4. Soften ice cream, to about a frozen yogurt texture and pour/spread on top of Oreo crush. Freeze for 2 hours.
5. Then spread fudge (slightly warmed) over top of frozen ice cream. Freeze for 2 hours. You can also add carmel sauce, peanuts, sea salt and other yummies.
6. Spread softened cool whip on top. Use whole container.
7. Crumble more Oreos on top for a "Storm of delish!"
8. Freeze again for 1 hour.

Gather the Tribe in for a fabulous Summer dessert!

Special thank you to Meredith, Tori, Caitlin, Maddie and Kyle for giving me permission to share your Angel Mother's Recipe.
I love you all!

Chocolate Walnut Crumb Bars

-By Gayle Tirri

- 1 Cup butter (2 sticks)
- 2 Cups flour
- 1/2 Cup sugar
- 1/4 tsp salt
- 2 Cups chocolate chips (12 oz package)
- 14 oz can sweetened condensed milk
- 1 tsp vanilla
- 1 Cup chopped walnuts

1. Preheat oven to 350 degrees.
2. Beat butter until creamy.
3. Beat in flour, sugar and salt until crumbly.
4. With floured fingers, press 2/3 crumb mix onto bottom of 9x13 greased pan. Reserve other 1/3 of mixture.
5. Bake in preheated 350 degree oven for 10 minutes.
6. Warm 1 1/2 bag chocolate chip morsels and condensed milk in a small pan over low heat.
7. Stir in vanilla.
8. Spread over hot crust.
9. To remaining mixture, add walnuts and the rest of the chocolate chip morsels. Stir and crumble on top of chocolate filling.
10. Bake 25 minutes and then cool on wire rack
11. Cut into squares or on the diagonal.

Texas Sheetcake

Camp Nannybones is a time for all of our sweet grandchildren to join us at our home for several days. Our time together is filled with joy, some hilarious moments, and the priceless wonder of making lasting memories. Every year is a new adventure, this year was go-karts for the big kids (yes, that's including me) and little electric rides for the babies. I try to cook and bake all their favorites and we eat and eat and then we sing and dance and swim and do crafts and act out melodramatic stories from the Bible. It is glorious chaos and we adore every single minute of being together. This year was a very quick four days.

Filled with dread for the moment of their departure, I could not sleep the night before. Finally, at 3:00 a.m., I climbed out of bed and decided to create a remedy for the sad of heart. I baked my Grand Littles' favorite dessert, Texas Sheet Cake, a rich chocolate concoction topped with fudgy icing. I spread the icing over the top and left it sitting on the kitchen counter to cool. My darlings woke up to the divine smell of fudgy chocolate drifting throughout the house, and exclaimed that I must love them more than anything in the world. They ate it for breakfast and asked me to pack some for their journey.

When we hugged, and kissed goodbye, I did not cry near as much this time. My heart is full when I think of their sweet faces as they tasted and shouted their hoorays for my love in baking them a cake at 3:00 a.m. That, my friend, is true love extraordinaire.

The Best Ever Texas Sheet Cake

This is our family favorite of all time. You can make this as quick as a wink, almost as soon as you hear them pull into the drive-way and get through the door! Mom Thelma, my wonderful mom-in-law, taught me how to make this cake. Hint* Mom taught me if you don't have sour cream add a teaspoon of white vinegar to the milk. Works every time!

- 1 Cup water
- 1 Cup butter (2 sticks)
- 3 Tbsp unsweetened cocoa powder
- 2 Cups all-purpose flour
- 2 Cups granulated sugar
- 1 tsp baking soda
- 1/2 tsp salt
- 1/2 Cup sour cream
- 2 large eggs
- 1 tsp vanilla extract

Frosting:
- 6 Tbsp milk
- 3 Tbsp unsweetened cocoa powder
- 1/2 Cup butter (1 stick)
- 3 3/4 Cups powdered sugar

The Best Ever Texas Sheet Cake, Cont.

1. Preheat oven to 350 degrees F and grease a 18x13" pan.
2. Add water, butter, and cocoa powder to a medium saucepan over medium heat. Bring mixture to a boil.
3. Meanwhile, in a separate bowl mix together the flour, sugar, baking soda and salt.
4. In another small bowl mix together the sour cream, eggs and vanilla.
5. Add sour cream/egg mixture to the flour mixture and mix until combined.
6. Once the chocolate mixture in the saucepan in boiling, remove it from heat and pour it into the batter. Mix until combined and no lumps remain.
7. Pour mixture into prepared pan and smooth with a spatula to make sure it is dispersed in an even layer.
8. Bake in preheated oven for 15-20 minutes or until set (mine is usually done around 15 minutes).
9. When the cake is about half-way through cooking, prepare the frosting.

For the Chocolate Sheet Cake Frosting:
1. Add milk, cocoa and butter to a saucepan. Bring mixture to a boil.
2. Once boiling, remove it from the heat and stir in powdered sugar. I like to beat the mixture with my hand-held mixer to get rid of any lumps.
3. Pour hot icing over hot cake. Use a spatula to spread it evenly over the cake. Allow frosting to set for about 10 minutes before eating.

The Rockiest Rocky Road Never Fail Bars

- 1 large package chocolate chips
- One small package butterscotch chips
- 1 Cup peanut butter (chunky or smooth)
- 1 regular package of miniature marshmallows

1. In a bowl, melt chips and peanut butter together in the microwave.
2. Stir in marshmallows and pour it into a pan to set.
3. Cut into bars after it is cool.

Hello Delish Dollies

- 1 Stick Butter
- 1 Cup Graham Cracker Crumbs
- 1 6 ounce package Cream Cheese
- 1 Cup Coconut
- 1 Cup Pecans
- 1 Cup Eagle Brand Milk

1. Preheat oven to 350 degrees.
2. Melt butter and sprinkle graham cracker crumbs evenly.
3. Layer ingredients in a dish and pour eagle brand milk over mixture.
4. Bake in oven at 350 degrees till golden brown.

Doris and the Rhubarb Robbery

I didn't steal it! At least I didn't really mean to steal it. I borrowed it. When I saw those six perfectly baked rhubarb pies that Doris had just pulled out of her oven resting on top of the stove, I knew I had to do something drastic. Doris and her husband Maurice did not just have a family, they had a tribe. Six girls and two boys, plus several adopted children and adults who claimed to belong to this extraordinary people. We all wanted to belong to them. Doris was legendary in many aspects of her life, raising her children who all are brilliant and amazing, and loving others like they were her own. This is just one of her gifts. Her laughter, the sparkle in her eyes, the look of sincere care when she listens and speaks with the wisdom of her well-lived life are all encounters to treasure. One of her biggest gifts, though, is her heart of grace and mercy, forgiving the trespasses of others. I thankfully confess to being one of those recipients of her mercy and forgiveness.

I had a previous engagement and could not be at the Gordon's family dinner that night. I was so disappointed because I knew there would not be one scrap left over of those rhubarb pies. While everyone else was occupied, I went to the kitchen and borrowed one of the pies. I fully intended to bring it back to the kitchen after I got back from my meeting and had a bite or two. I slipped the rhubarb pie into the top drawer of the dresser, on top of my shoes, where I knew it would be safe until I arrived back home.

It was after midnight when I finally pulled out the drawer. There it was safely hidden away, that borrowed rhubarb pie. I cannot tell you how it happened, maybe it was the striking of midnight, maybe it was the pie fairy that overcame my good senses. But after a few bites, and before I knew it, I had eaten that entire pie all by myself.

The next morning at breakfast I was guilt-laden and full as a tick.

Mother Doris began serving the platters of hot delicious food and then declared, "I must be getting old. I was sure I made six pies yesterday but last night we ate all of the pies. I am so sorry, Nancy. I know you were looking forward to having some rhubarb pie." I was horrified but knew I must confess my sin, so I told them about the rhubarb robbery and of my sincere intention of having a few bites and putting the rest back. A sudden silence fell over the table, then we all began howling with laughter until some of us had tears streaming.

The family still loves me, and, thankfully, I still belong to them. We have stayed close and navigated our lives through weddings, births and the deaths of those we long to hold but know we will see again. Within the chronicles of these days we have found the sweetest solace in sharing our joys and sorrows, always finding grace and comfort in the songs we write and sing, and worshipping God together. It is what makes us family.

Mom Gordon & Her Rhubarb Pie

- 3 to 4 Cups of Rhubarb
- 1 1/2 Cup sugar
- 1 egg beaten with a fork
- 2 Tbsp butter (melted)
- Dash of salt
- 2 Tbsp flour

1. Preheat oven to 425 degrees.
2. Wash and prepare rhubarb. Cut rhubarb into 1 inch pieces.
3. Put rhubarb in a bowl then add remaining ingredients. Mix well.
4. Prepare crust.
5. Put crust in pie pan, pour all ingredients into the pan then add top crust.
6. Bake at 425 degrees for 15 minutes.
7. Then lower temperature to 350 degrees and bake the pie until golden brown.
8. Serve warm!

This pie is addictive as I wrote about in the short story "Doris and the Rhubarb Robbery" in my confession of eating the entire pie.
I never told my mom, she would have been horrified, and even more so because I enjoyed every bite and to this day I feel no regrets.

Sticky Date Pudding

-Recipe by my Austrialian friend Sue Downs with Lillia Celobski

- 1/2 Cup dates, pitted and chopped
- 1 tsp bicarbonate of soda
- 5 Tbsp + 1 tsp butter
- 1/2 Cup caster sugar (make caster sugar by putting granulated sugar in a blender, blend for 3 or 4 minutes until sugar has become fine powder.)
- 2 eggs
- 1/2 Cup self raising flour
- 1/2 tsp vanilla essence

1. Preheat oven to 350 degrees.
2. Mix dates and bicarbonate of soda. Pour 1 1/4 cups boiling water over dates and leave to stand.
3. Cream butter and sugar until pale then add eggs one at a time, beating well after each addition.
4. Gently fold in flour, stir in date mixture and vanilla.
5. Pour into well buttered cake tin and bake at 350 degrees for 30-40 minutes.
6. Serve with butterscotch sauce.

Butterscotch Sauce

- 2/3 Cup brown sugar
- 2/3 Cup cream
- 1 vanilla bean, split
- 1/4 Cup butter

1. Combine sugar, cream, vanilla bean and butter in a pot.
2. Bring to a boil and simmer for 5 minutes.
3. Set aside until ready to reheat and pour over pudding.
4. Discard vanilla bean.

Cinnamon Sour Cream Cake

-Richard M's momma baked this beautiful cake Christmas or Thanksgiving mornings. It is perfect in every way.

- 3/4 Cup walnuts chopped
- 1 tsp cinnamon
- 1 Tbsp sugar
- 1 Cup butter
- 1 1/4 Cups sugar
- 2 eggs
- 1 Cup of sour cream
- 2 Cups of flour
- 1 1/2 tsp baking powder
- 1/2 tsp baking soda
- 1 tsp vanilla

1. Preheat oven to 350 degrees.
2. Combine walnuts, cinnamon, 1 Tbsp sugar and set aside.
3. Combine butter, sugar, eggs and sour cream.
4. Sift flour, baking soda and baking powder. Pour into cream mixture.
5. Add vanilla, blend well.
6. Spoon half of the batter into bunt pan, then sprinkle half of the cinnamon mixture.
7. Add remaining batter then top with the rest of the cinnamon mix.
8. Place in cold oven, set temperature at 350 degrees and bake 55 minutes until golden brown.

Serve this cinnamon sour cream cake warm from the oven. Perfect with a cup of hot tea or a cuppa. It is an extraordinary way to start a holiday!

Grandma Thelma's Chocolate Frosted Graham Crackers

- 3 Tbsp butter melted
- 2 Tbsp Hershey's 100% naturally unsweetened cocoa
- 2-1/2 Cups powdered sugar
- 1/4 Cup milk
- 1 tsp vanilla

1. Mix ingredients in bowl until smooth and then spread on graham crackers.
2. Serves 15 hefty graham crackers!

Saint Jean's Strawberries & Crust

- 3 Cups sifted flour
- 1 tsp salt
- 1 Cup shortening
- 1 egg
- 6 Tbsp water

Strawberries:
- 4-6 baskets of strawberries
- 2.5 Cups sugar to 6 Cups strawberries
- Whipped cream

Guaranteed there will be no leftovers!

1. Sift flour with salt.
2. Cut shortening into flour.
3. Beat egg with water and sprinkle over flour mixture.
4. Mix gently.
5. Roll out pie crust on cookie sheet.
6. Bake crust for 15-20 minutes until golden brown.

Strawberries:

1. Prepare strawberries by washing, slicing in half and adding in desired sugar.
2. Let the mixture sit out at room temperature.
3. Remove half of the strawberries, set aside.
4. Puree remaining strawberries then add back in the rest of the strawberries.
5. In a serving bowl, break off generous pieces of crust, ladle strawberries over crust and repeat this process.

I find 2 layers is plenty, but you can keep going if you like! Then top the layers with vanilla ice cream and another drizzle of strawberries. Then for the grand finale, place a huge liberal dollop of whipped cream!

The Peach Cobbler

It was Thanksgiving. We were in Houston staying with Daniel and Jan Calk. They were helping Jan's parents, James and Ima Kilgore, pastor a large, flourishing church. With hundreds of members, it was quite normal to be called upon to help people at a moment's notice. Daniel and Jan were premiere pastors and loved people without reserve. They had a darling little boy the same age as our little Mindy. Christopher and Mindy were fast friends and had the time of their lives playing and making fun adventures.

Jan is a fabulous cook (not surprising at all since she came from a legacy of the best Southern cooks known to man). Jan decided to whip up one of her fast and fabulous peach cobblers. She said she would teach me the secret to her delicious and super easy cobbler. She began throwing stuff in the bowl so fast I could barely keep up. She had it all mixed and ready, when she received a call from a church member going through a crisis.

Jan left that innocent bowl of cobbler topping sitting out on the counter while she took her call. I thought I should just have a little taste to make sure it was sweet enough. That was a mistake.

When Jan got off the phone and came back into the kitchen I was standing over the nearly empty bowl, spoon poised in the air, going after another bite. There was no denying what had happened. The cobbler topping had nearly disappeared. I was in a state of shock, both at being caught and at the rate at which the topping had gone down my throat. My mouth hung open. How could I have eaten all of that so quickly? Jan started laughing so hard she was crying, and so was I.

We worked together in her kitchen that Thanksgiving to whip up another batch of topping, and I paid more attention that time to her ancient secrets that made this cobbler so divine.

Jan's peach cobbler is addictive. Just beware. When you are in the process of making the batter for the topping, do not leave it unprotected! Put that cobbler together and place it in the oven immediately to avoid pre-baked decimation by starving friends.

Jan's Peach Cobbler

- 1 Cup sugar
- 1 Cup self-rising flour
- Pinch of cinnamon
- 1 Cup milk
- 1 stick of butter, melted
- 1 large can of peaches
- 1/2 Cup sugar

1. Preheat oven to 350 degrees.
2. Mix together 1 cup sugar, 1 cup self-rising flour and a pinch of cinnamon. Stir well.
3. Next, add in 1 cup milk, stir and combine
4. Melt a stick of butter in a pan and pour the batter over the melted butter.
5. Add a large can of peaches, do not stir.
6. Bake 1 hour in 350 degree oven.

Grandma Faithy's Famous Bread Pudding

-Authenticated by her daughter, Hope King

- 14-15 pieces of day old white bread
- 2 large eggs
- 1/2 Cup of sugar
- 1 can Carnation, Milnot or Pet milk
- 1 Cup whole milk
- 1 small carton half and half
- A dash of salt
- 2 tsp cinnamon
- Optional: 1 Tbsp vanilla

1. Preheat oven to 350 degrees.
2. Crumble day old bread into a 9x13 pan.
3. In a mixing bowl beat: eggs, sugar, carnation milk, whole milk, half and half, salt, cinnamon and vanilla.
4. Beat good and then pour over the bread.
5. Let sit for 5 minutes to absorb the liquid.
6. Bake at 350 degrees for 30-45 minutes, or until custard is set but still a little wobbly and edges and top of the bread has browned.
7. Remove from the oven and let cool for 10 minutes. Then drizzle the vanilla sauce over top. Vanilla sauce found on page 172,

Grandma Faithy Keller has lived a long legacy of faithfulness and loving God. She lost her husband when she was a young woman and still had children to raise. She was courageous, always elegant, and classy. She knows how to make a seriously fabulous Bread Pudding!

This Bread Pudding could bring world peace, especially if beautiful Grandma Faithy was serving it! One smile from her gorgeous face and it would melt down every sword into spoons and plowshares into platters.

Kennedy Kate's Best Peanut Butter Cookies

- 1 Cup unsalted butter
- 1 Cup crunchy peanut butter
- 1 Cup white sugar
- 1 Cup brown sugar
- 2 eggs
- 2.5 Cups all purpose flour
- 1 tsp baking powder
- 1/2 tsp salt
- 1.5 tsp baking soda

1. Preheat oven to 375 degrees.
2. Cream butter, peanut butter and sugars together in a bowl.
3. Beat in eggs.
4. In a separate bowl, sift flour, baking powder, baking soda and salt.
5. Stir into butter mixture.
6. Put dough in refrigerator for 1 hour.
7. Roll dough into 1 inch balls and put on baking sheets. Flatten each ball with a fork, making a crisscross pattern. Bake in a preheated 375 degree oven for about 10 minutes or until cookies begin to brown.

No worries on how to store these cookies. Every time Kennedy makes a batch of her magical peanut butter cookies there is never any left to store!
She has been baking delightful treats for her family since she was 6 years old! #hermotherschild

Bread

"I will always look to you, as you stand beside me and protect me from fear."
Psalms 16:8

Nannybones Outrageous Yeast Rolls

- 1 Cup of milk
- 3 Tbsp shortening
- 1/2 Cup of sugar
- 1/2 Tbsp salt
- 1 pkg. quick rising yeast
- 2 Cups of flour
- 1 egg

1. Heat oven to 400 degrees.
2. Bring milk to a boil, add in shortening, sugar and salt. Set aside until cool.
3. Dissolve yeast in 1/2 to 3/4 cup of very warm water, but not too hot (this will kill the rise of the yeast). Start adding in flour and beat.
4. Beat egg and add to flour and yeast mixture.
5. Keep adding in flour until gooey.
6. Put on floured surface and knead. Then put into a large bowl (I butter the bottom and sides) and let rise for 1 1/2 to 2 hours.
7. Once risen, roll dough out, divide in half first, put melted butter onto rolled dough and cut into pie shapes. Roll from large end to small.
8. Bake until light brown.

I usually quadruple this recipe. It makes people smile upon the very first bite.

yeast Rolls

— Tootie —

Tootie

Our family is addicted to my outrageous yeast rolls. The process takes time and patience, but is well worth it. I usually quadruple my recipe to have plenty for the family (25 at the moment) but also to share with my neighbors, my friends–and my enemies!

One particular Thanksgiving I made an excessively huge batch of rolls. I used 12 cookie sheets to put the rolls on to rise. When they were quite fluffy and ready to bake, I noticed several of the rolls had gone missing. I thought that was odd, but with 15 grandchildren, nothing is ever a surprise. I just assumed the children had taken a few of the raw rolls to play with.

Later that evening our pug dog Tootie, the cutest dog ever, started acting strange. By 11:00 p.m., Tootie could barely walk, and was actually falling over onto her back, her feet sticking up in the air, with her tongue hanging out. I honestly thought she had gotten into some whiskey or sleeping pills or some kind of drug. I was petrified. My husband and our son found a veterinary clinic open. On Thanksgiving night the cost was exorbitant, but we thought she might die.

The vet and his assistant took her back to examine her. After a bit, the vet came out and showed my husband and son a white substance on the end of a tongue depressor. He said, " I don't know for sure what this is, but your dog is full of it, and it smells like yeast!"

And that's exactly what it was. Probably 10 raw yeast rolls the kids had played with, and then just dropped them when they were tired of them. Tootie loved them and ate every single one of them!

They had to pump her stomach. They were amazed she had not blown up with the quick rising yeast working double time. They put her on an IV for 24 hours. When we finally were able to bring her home, that dog was still intoxicated from the fermented yeast and unable to walk a straight line. She was so drunk she could barely stay upright. We put her to bed and she finally slept it off.

And those were the MOST expensive yeast rolls I have ever made!

Pumpkin Bread

- 3 Cups of sugar
- 1 Cup of oil
- 1 1/2 tsp salt
- 1 tsp nutmeg
- 1 tsp cinnamon

(or may use 2 tsp pumpkin pie spice)

- 2/3 Cup water
- 2 Cups pureed pumpkin
- 1 1/2 Cups raisins
- 3 1/2 Cups flour
- 2 tsp baking soda

(sift the soda into the flour)

1. Heat oven to 350 degrees
2. Mix everything together in a large bowl.
3. Pour into non-greased, non-stick loaf pans. This recipe makes 2 or 3 loaves.
4. Bake at 350 for 1 hour, test with toothpick to make sure it is done.

Aunt Shirley (she was Richard M's favorite) made pumpkin bread for the family every Fall. She was the epitome of goodness. She worked as a child advocate and loved everyone beyond expression. She was mom to a tribe of kids. Becky (Bec Bec the Barbecue sauce cooking and baking guru) was her girl.

Jewish Coffee Cake

Cake Mix:
- 1 box Duncan Hines yellow cake mix
- 1/2 Cup buttery flavored oil
- 1 Cup water
- 4 eggs
- 1 1/2 packages instant vanilla pudding mix
- 1 tsp vanilla extract

Filling:
- 1/2 Cup nuts
- 1/2 Cup sugar
- 1 1/2 tsp cinnamon

1. Heat oven to 350 degrees
2. Beat cake mix ingredients for 4 minutes.
3. Prepare pan.
4. Prepare filling.
5. Pour half of the cake mix into pan, sprinkle filling over this, then add remaining cake mix.
6. Bake at 350 degrees for 45 minutes to an hour, depending on your oven.
7. Test for doneness around 45 minutes by inserting a toothpick in the center of cake.

This bread is so good on Christmas morning!

Blueberry Nut Bread

- 1 package Duncan Hines blueberry muffin mix
- 1/3 Cup chopped nuts, pecans or walnuts
- 3 Tbsp sugar
- 1/2 Cup & 1 Tbsp water
- 1 Cup of blueberries

1. Preheat oven to 375 degrees.
2. Grease and flour a 9x5x3 pan.
3. Empty blueberries into strainer, wash under cold running water and set aside to drain.
4. In a medium bowl, combine all ingredients and then add blueberries.
5. Spread batter into prepared pan and bake at 375 degrees for 30-35 minutes.
6. Test with toothpick and let cool for 10 minutes.

Blueberry Coffee Cake

- 1 package Duncan Hines blueberry muffin mix
- 2 Tbsp cooking oil
- 1 egg
- 1/2 Cup water
- 1/3 Cup brown sugar
- 1 tsp cinnamon
- 1/2 to 1 Cup of blueberries

1. Heat oven to 350 degrees.
2. Empty blueberries into strainer and set aside to drain.
3. Pour oil into an 8 or 9 inch square or round pan and make sure oil coats pan evenly.
4. Put muffin mix, egg and water into pan. Stir with a fork until blended (about 1 minute).
5. Sprinkle drained blueberries, brown sugar and cinnamon over batter.
6. Use a fork to fold into batter just enough to create a marbled effect.
7. Scrape sides and spread batter evenly in pan.
8. Bake at 350 degrees for 25-35 minutes until coffee cake tests done with a toothpick.
9. Use a knife to loosen cake from sides, cut and serve directly from pan.

Lakelie's Cataclysmic Cinnamon Rolls

Dough:

- 2 Cups whole milk
- 1/2 Cup vegetable oil
- 1/2 Cup sugar
- 2 packages active dry yeast (.25 ounce packets)
- 4 Cups (plus 1/2 cup extra separated and set aside) all purpose flour
- 1/2 tsp heaping baking powder
- 1/2 tsp scant baking soda
- 2 tsp salt

Filling:

- Loads of melted butter (no less than 1 1/2 cups)
- 1 Cup sugar
- 1 Cup brown sugar
- Generous sprinkling of cinnamon
- Toasted pecans (optional)

Vanilla Frosting:

- 1/2 bag powdered sugar
- 1/4 Cup whole milk
- 2 Tbsp melted butter
- 1/4 Cup cream cheese softened
- Pinch of salt
- 2 tsp vanilla

Lakelie's Cataclysmic Cinnamon Rolls Cont.

In medium saucepan:

Heat the milk, vegetable oil, and sugar over medium heat to just below a boil. Set aside and cool .

Sprinkle the yeast on top and let it sit for one minute. Then add in 4 cups of flour. Stir until just combined, then cover with a clean kitchen towel and set aside in a warm, draft free place for one hour. On hot summer days I put this mixture out on a bench on our porch, it rises perfectly! I think it might be the birds that chirp and sing, that must make that pan of dough want to rise up and shout Hallelujah!

After 1 hour, remove the towel and add the baking powder, baking soda, salt, and the remaining 1/2 cup of flour. Stir thoroughly to combine, or use a standing mixer with the dough hook attachment. Use the dough right away, or place in a mixing bowl, cover and refrigerate for up to 3 days, punching down the dough if it rises to the top of the bowl. (Note: Dough is easier to work with if it's been chilled for at least an hour before you use it.)

To assemble the rolls, remove the dough from the pan and cut in half. On a floured baking surface, roll half the dough into a large rectangle, about 24x10 inches. The dough should be rolled very thin. Do not slack on this instruction. I thought I could get by and make a thicker roll but it made baking the cinnamon roll difficult for it to be thoroughly baked through and through.

To make the filling, combine the white sugar and brown sugar in a mixing bowl. Set aside. Pour half of the melted butter over the surface of the dough. Use your fingers (my preference) or the back of a spoon to spread the butter evenly. Generously sprinkle ground cinnamon and half of the sugar mixture over the butter. If adding nuts, now is the time.

Lakelie's Cataclysmic Cinnamon Rolls Cont.

Beginning at the end farthest from you, roll the rectangle tightly towards you. Use both hands and work slowly, being careful to keep the roll tight. When you reach the end, pinch the seam together and flip the roll so that the seam is face down.

Slip a cutting board underneath the roll and with a sharp knife, make 1 1/2-inch slices. One log will produce about 10 rolls. Place the sliced rolls in a buttered pan, being careful not to over crowd. Repeat the rolling, sugar, butter process with the other half of the dough and one more buttered pan.

Preheat the oven to 375° cover both pans with a kitchen towel and set aside to rise on the countertop for at least 20 minutes before baking. Remove the towel and bake for 15 to 18 minutes, until golden brown. Do not allow the rolls to become too brown.

While the rolls are baking, make the icing: in a large bowl, whisk together the powdered sugar, milk, butter, cream cheese and salt. Add the vanilla and whisk until very smooth. The icing should be somewhat thick but still pourable.

Remove the rolls from the oven when done. Immediately drizzle the icing over the top of the hot cinnamon rolls, making sure to get all around the edges and over the top. Serve hot.

NOTE: I know this cinnamon roll recipe seems very complicated and time consuming but I promise you after you taste the first roll you will be so glad you made the effort, and so will your family.

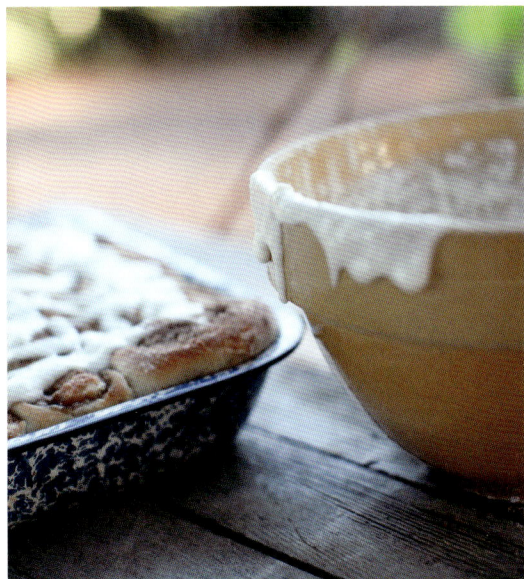

Lakelie's Cataclysmic Cinnamon Rolls

Pecan Breakfast Bread

- 2 cans Pillsbury Refrigerator Quick Crescent Rolls
- 2 Tbsp butter, softened
- 1/2 Cup sugar
- 1/2 tsp cinnamon
- 1/4 Cup chopped pecans

Topping:
- 2 Tbsp honey
- 1/4 Cup powdered sugar
- 2 Tbsp butter
- 1 tsp vanilla extract
- 1/4 Cup pecan halves

1. Heat oven to 375 degrees.
2. Unroll crescent dough and separate into triangles.
3. Spread each triangle with butter
4. In a bowl, combine sugar, cinnamon and pecans. Sprinkle mixture over triangles.
5. Roll up each triangle starting at wide end and rolling to the opposite point of the triangle.
6. Place rolls point side down in greased 9x5 pan forming 2 layers of 8 rolls each.
7. Bake at 375 degrees for 35-50 minutes, or until golden brown and center is done.
8. Remove from pan at once.
9. To make topping: combine all ingredients except pecans in a saucepan. Bring to a boil, stirring consistently.
10. Stir in pecans, cool slightly.
11. Place crescent rolls right side up and drizzle with topping.

Tip: Bread may be made ahead of time, sliced and reheated at 350 degrees for 15 minutes.

Cheese Breakfast Biscuits

- 8 or 10 ounces Cheddar Cheese, grated
- 1 pound sausage
- 3 cups Bisquick

1. Preheat oven to 375 degrees.
2. Mix ingredients together and form in to small balls, approximately 1 inch each.
3. Place on cookie sheet spaced out, not touching each other.
4. Bake 15 minutes at 375 degrees.

Note: You may want to freeze and pop into the oven anytime. Be sure to thaw some and allow adequate spacing between each biscuit.

My Son Richard's Favorite Biscuits

- 2 Cups regular flour
- 4 tsp baking powder
- 1/2 tsp salt
- 1 tsp sugar
- 1/2 Cup shortening
- 1 large egg
- Sweet milk

1. Preheat oven to 450 degrees.
2. Sift first 4 ingredients together.
3. Work shortening in by hand.
4. Place egg in measuring cup and add milk to make one cupful.
5. Add milk & egg to dry ingredients, stir in with spoon.
6. Shape into soft lump and put on a floured board.
7. Cut and shape into desired size and bake until golden brown.

William Cook's Sicilian Stuffing

- 1 1/2 Cup butter
- 1/3 Cup olive oil
- 1 1/2 Cups chopped celery
- 1 1/2 Cups chopped onions
- 1 Pan of cornbread
- 1 Box of seasoned cornbread mix
- 2 Tbsp sage
- Season with garlic salt and pepper
- 3 to 4 Cups of seasoned turkey broth
- 1 pound mild Italian sausage
- 1 pound hot sausage
- 1 pound sage sausage
- 1/2-1 pound smoked sausage

Confession: Sometimes this is all I want at our holiday dinners. It's a meal all by itself. I just put a little of my homemade cranberry sauce and it is a feast!

1. In a large pot, melt butter and add in olive oil, chopped celery, chopped onions, Italian sausage, hot sausage, sage sausage and smoke sausage.
2. I use a spatula and chop thru the sausage mixture as it cooks down with the onion and celery mixture. Cook this on medium to medium low heat for 15-20 minutes.
3. Once cooked, add in 6 cups fresh crumbled cornbread, 12 oz box of seasoned cornbread, 2 Tbsp of sage, garlic salt and pepper to taste.
4. Mix all ingredients together.
5. Pour seasoned turkey broth "magical potion" over dressing mixture until moistened but not too wet!
6. Place stuffing into baking dish. Cover with foil. Bake for 45 minutes at 350 degrees.
7. Remove foil and brown for 5 minutes.

Note: Sometimes I add hot links to give it a kick!

Critical facts!

1. The day before, you need to make the cornbread, boil the turkey neck and giblets in seasoned water (garlic salt, garlic pepper, onion soup mix)...till neck is soft. Refrigerate overnight. Clean meat off neck and add to broth, heat turkey broth mixture (might need to add chicken or turkey broth).
2. I use any extra to season my gravy and sometimes, if I have potato juice in the freezer, I add that..

Mexican Cornbread

-By Sherry Liles

- 2 boxes Jiffy Corn Muffin Mix
- 1 stick butter, melted
- 1 Cup sour cream
- 1 can cream corn
- Tad of sugar (which I don't usually add, this recipe is sweet enough with the corn)

1. Preheat over to 350 degrees.
2. Melt butter and add in medium sized bowl.
3. Drain the juice from the can of whole kernel corn.
4. Add the can of creamed corn and whole kernel corn. Mix everything together.
5. Add both boxes of Jiffy Corn Muffin Mix and mix well.
6. Optional: add the sugar and mix well.
7. Add the sour cream and mix well.
8. Pour into a greased 9x9 casserole dish .
9. Bake for 50-55 minutes until top is golden brown and knife comes out mostly clean in the center

My sweet lifelong friend Sherry Liles is one of the best southern cooks I know.
One year for my birthday she hand wrote an entire book of her favorite recipes.
It is a treasure in my cookbook collection.
The one thing I have learned in my 70 years is that you cannot make old friends, so celebrate them, tell them you love them.
Sherry is pure gold and forever in my heart.

Double Cornbread—Double Delish

- 1 Cup corn meal
- 8 oz carton sour cream
- 3 eggs
- 1/3 Cup oil
- 1 Cup creamed corn
- 1/4 tsp salt

1. Preheat oven to 350 degrees
2. Mix all ingredients together.
3. Put mixture in greased iron skillet or baking dish. (I put the iron skillet in the oven and let it get hot, take it out and add the oil and then put it back in the oven until hot, then pour cornbread mix into skillet. It makes the outside of the cornbread crisp, although not too healthy for arteries!)
4. Please use extreme caution if you choose to use this method, you can burn yourself if you are not very careful.
5. Bake for 45 minutes or until golden brown.

I double this recipe, save and freeze it so I can use it in my stuffing. It is unexpectedly flavorful and will bring a whole new dimension to the taste and enjoyment of your special celebrations and holiday dinners.

French Toast Souffle

- 1 Bread loaf (challah or french)
- 2/3 Cup half & half
- 8 oz. cream cheese, softened
- 6 eggs
- 3/4 Cup Maple Syrup
- 1 tsp Vanilla
- 1 1/2 Cups milk
- 1/4 Cup Powdered Sugar

1. Coat a 13x9 baking dish with spray.
2. Line dish with bread slices.
3. Beat cream cheese until smooth. Add eggs & beat well.
4. Add milk, half & half, 3/4 cup syrup and vanilla until smooth.
5. Pour mixture over bread, cover and refrigerate overnight.
6. Before baking, let stand for 30 minutes.
7. Preheat oven to 375 degrees. Bake until golden, usually 39 minutes.
8. Dust with powdered sugar or serve individually.
9. Serve with fresh fruit and nuts.

Note: Can be made immediately, just soak bread thoroughly.

Soup

"I give you peace, the kind of peace only I can give. It isn't like the peace this world can give. So don't be worried or afraid."

John 14:27

Roasted Butternut Squash Soup

- 1 Medium Butternut Squash (3 pounds) peeled, seeded, and cut into 1 1/2 inch chunks
- 1 1/2 pounds Golden Delicious Apples, peeled, cored and chopped
- 3 medium shallots, peeled and quartered
- 1/4 Cup vegetable oil
- salt and pepper
- 4 Cups chicken broth
- 1 Tbsp maple syrup
- 1 tsp ground nutmeg
- 1/4 Cup heavy cream

1. After removing the stem and root end, cut the squash in half crosswise where the thinner neck meets the thicker base. This is an easy way to prepare the squash.
2. Adjust oven rack to middle position and Preheat oven to 450 degrees.
3. Toss squash, apples, shallots, oil, 1 tsp salt and 1/2 tsp pepper in large bowl, then arrange in single layer in large roasting pan.
4. Roast, stirring occasionally, until vegetables are golden brown and softened, about 45 minutes.
5. Add 1/2 cup broth to pan and scrape up any browned bits with wooden spoon.
6. Return it to oven and cook until liquid has reduced and vegetables are glazed, about 5 minutes.
7. Working in 2 batches, puree squash mixture and remaining broth in blender until smooth.
8. Transfer pureed squash mixture to large saucepan and stir in syrup, nutmeg and cream.
9. Bring soup to a simmer over medium-low heat, adding 1/4 cup water at a time as necessary to adjust consistency.
10. Serve.

Note: Soup can be refrigerated in an airtight container for 3 days.

Cheese Soup

- 1 stick butter
- 1/2 Cup minced green onion
- 2 Cups minced celery
- 1 Cup flour
- 4 pounds Velveeta cheese
- 4 Cups boiling water
- 4 Cups chicken broth
- 4 Cups evaporated milk
- 2 Cups milk
- Salt and pepper to taste

1. Saute vegetables in butter until slightly brown.
2. Scald milk and broth together.
3. Add flour to vegetables, mixing well.
4. Add boiling water and scalded milk and broth. Stir well.
5. Tear cheese into small pieces and add into mixture.
6. Put into double boiler and cook on medium heat until cheese melts.
7. Soup will curdle if it is cooked too fast.

Cowgirl Hamburger Soup

-Verla Simmons gave me this recipe 40 years ago. My darling love of 52 years Richard M. loves it, especially when I add a piece of cheese on the top.

- 1 pound hamburger
- 1 chopped onion
- 1 Bay leaf
- Jalapeño peppers
- Frozen vegetables (corn, carrots, green beans)
- 1 head cabbage chopped
- 2 large cans of tomatoes
- Salt and Pepper to taste

1. Saute onions and hamburger and cook till done.
2. Put this and all other ingredients into large pan or crock pot.
3. Cook at least 1 hour, or until everything is tender.
4. Serve with cornbread or Mexican cornbread.

Boo's Chili

-Beulah Hill made this wonderful Chili in 1975 in Maldon, Missouri.

- 1 pound ground sirloin
- 1 Pound pinto beans (cooked)
- 1 chopped yellow onion
- 1 tsp salt
- 1 tsp pepper
- 1 package chili mix
- 2 small cans tomato sauce

1. Brown hamburger with onion, salt and pepper.
2. Beans should be cooked in advance.
3. Add all ingredients to cooked beans and stir in chili mix and tomato sauce.
4. Let simmer for 1 hour or cook in crock pot all day.

This is easy and simple to make, it is a good Recipe to teach your Kids.

Corn Chowder

- 4 Tbsp butter
- 3 Tbsp chopped onion
- 1 quart milk
- 4 Cups diced potatoes
- 2 cans cream corn
- Salt and Pepper to taste

1. In a heavy pan, melt butter and add onions and saute until soft.
2. Add milk and potatoes and boil until tender.
3. Add corn and seasonings
4. Add ham, if desired.
5. Serve with cornbread.

Potato Soup for the win

- 6 Cups sliced potatoes
- 1/2 Cups sliced carrots
- 6 pieces bacon
- 1 Cup chopped onion
- 1 Cup sliced celery
- 1 1/2 tsp salt
- 1/4 tsp pepper
- 1 tsp kitchen crack (also known as Penzeys Sandwich Sprinkle)
- 2 Cups milk
- 2 Cups half and half
- Shredded cheddar cheese

1. Cook potatoes and carrots until tender.
2. Saute bacon until crisp, drain and crumble.
3. Saute onion and celery in 2 tsp bacon fat.
4. Combine all ingredients, simmer 30 minutes.

Chicken Gumbo

- 2 pounds chicken breast
- 6 Tbsp flour
- 4 Tbsp crisco
- 1/4 tsp salt
- 1 tsp red pepper
- 1 tsp black pepper
- 1 Tbsp parsley
- 1/2 Cup diced onion
- 1 bunch green onions, chopped (save for topping)
- 1 clove garlic
- 1 tsp or more Gumbo File'

1. Place chicken in pot, fill with enough water to cover chicken. Allow chicken to cook at least 30 minutes. Set aside until cool. Remove chicken meat, shred and set aside. Discard skin and bones.
2. Brown flour in crisco until medium or dark brown (it should have a nutty brown hue).
3. You must use a low temperature or flour will burn, this takes 1-2 hours.
4. When brown, add salt, pepper, parsley, diced onion and garlic. Let simmer for 5 minutes, stirring constantly.
5. Add 4 pints hot water or hot chicken broth.
6. Then add shredded chicken. Sometimes I add chopped okra and hot sausage.
7. Stir in File' and turn heat to low for 10 minutes.
8. Add green onions.
9. Add Tabasco if desired.

Note: Traditionally served with potato salad and bread.

Cheers to the Cook!

Chicken Gumbo

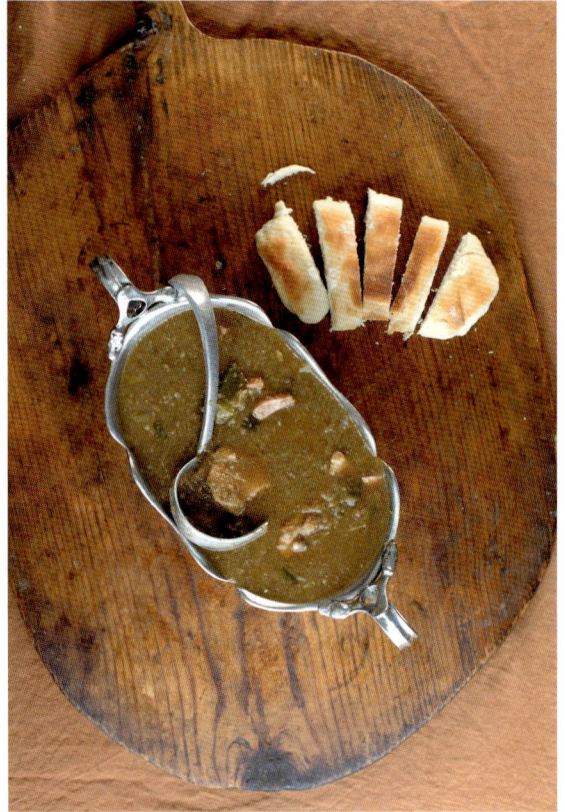

White Bean Chili

-By Donna Frost

- 5 Cups chopped cooked chicken
- 3-15 ounce cans Great Northern beans drained
- 1-32 ounce box chicken broth
- 1-16 ounce jar mild salsa
- 18 ounce package Monterey Jack cheese with peppers, cubed
- 2 tsp ground cumin
- Cheddar cheese
- Sour Cream
- Jalapeños

1. In a quart electric slow cooker, combine chicken, beans, broth, salsa, cheese and cumin. Cover and cook on high for 3 hours, stirring occasionally.
2. Reduce heat to low.
3. Garnish with cheddar cheese, sour cream and jalapenos if desired. Serve with corn chips.

Donna is one of the most celebrated interior designers of the Dallas Metroplex. Her husband Darrell is her go to person for the precision placement of 30 feet tall window treatments and other phenomenal feats. We had the best time staying in their splendid home and felt so loved and spoiled by the delicious dinners they cooked up in their dreamy kitchen. Here's to many more dear friends!

My French Onion Soup

It was my first try at making French onion soup. I found the coolest bowls with matching saucers. The finishing touch was the French writing on the side of the bowl that said "Bon-Appetite". With great anticipation, I went to the store and purchased everything I needed to make the perfect French onion soup from scratch for our dinner that night.

We were pastoring a church in the San Francisco Bay Area and raising our tribe of four children. It was fun, challenging, and exhausting. Throughout those busy years, it was our joy to entertain and host many ministers, pastors, missionaries and their families. This particular evening, we had a missionary staying with us. We looked forward to hearing about his thrilling adventures on the mission field.

My soup turned out perfect and was a complete success. I was so excited I could hardly wait to serve it up for our special dinner. Everyone was happily eating when our visiting missionary suddenly began choking on the thick cheese that topped the French onion soup. Not knowing where to look or what to do, our embarrassed children simply lowered their eyes. I looked at my husband with terror. He looked back at me mouthing the words, "What should I do?"

All at once, the choking man leaped out of his seat and ran out the patio door, my husband following close on his heels. I watched as Richard M. tried to reach in and grab hold of the end of the long rope of cheese coming from the throat of the hysterical, terrified missionary. The children and I ran out of the dining room, through the kitchen and down the hallway with tears streaming down our faces. We alternated between nervous laughter, weeping, and praying to God, the Almighty Deliverer from Sin and Sticky Cheese Goo, to help our Dad save the choking minister from my French onion soup.

Just as the minister began turning grotesque shades of blue and purplish gray and making curdled sounds, my hero husband gave the cheese a giant yank and the missionary was able to catch a breath of air. His countenance immediately returned to its natural color and an expression of liberated relief took over his face.

He was supposed to have stayed with us a few extra days due to some cancellations in his schedule, but I guess he called and found a place somewhere to minister. He said he had to get on the road to his next meeting.

We helped him pack his car. We sent snacks and sweets, but no soup, and no cheese.

That was the first and the last time I ever made French onion soup. I almost experience PTSD when I think about that whole horrific cheesy debacle.

While I am including the recipe in this book, I do not recommend that you fix it or serve it to your guests, especially missionaries, ministers or pastors. We seem to be in short supply of them these days.

Cheesy Onion Soup

WARNING: be cautious when serving to priests, pastors or missionaries. May serve without cheese as precautionary measure.

- 1/2 Cup unsalted butter
- 2 Tbsp olive oil
- 4 Cups sliced red onions
- 4 10.5 oz cans beef broth
- 1/2 tsp kitchen crack
- 1 tsp dried thyme
- 1 pinch garlic salt and pepper to taste
- 4 slices French bread
- 4 slices Provolone cheese
- 2 slices Swiss cheese, diced
- 1/4 Cup grated Parmesan cheese

1. Melt butter with olive oil in an 8 quart stock pot on medium heat.
2. Add onions and continually stir until tender and translucent. Do not brown the onions.
3. Add beef broth and thyme. Season with garlic salt and pepper, add kitchen crack and simmer for 30 minutes.
4. Ladle soup into oven safe serving bowls and place one slice of bread on top of each (bread may be broken into pieces if you prefer).
5. Layer each slice of bread with a slice of provolone, 1/2 slice diced Swiss cheese and 1 Tbsp Parmesan cheese.
6. Place bowls on cookie sheet and broil in the preheated oven until cheese bubbles and browns slightly.

Casseroles & My Favorite Dishes

"Then we which are alive and remain shall be caught up together with them in the clouds, to meet the Lord in the air: and so shall we ever be with the Lord."

1 Thessalonians 4:17

Meatballs Magnificent

- 5 pounds Ground Sirloin
- 5 pounds Ground Pork (seasoned)
- 5 pounds Veal
- 1 Cup shredded Romano cheese
- 4 to 5 eggs
- 1/2 to 3/4 Cup tomato sauce
- 5 slices of white bread (cut in pieces)
- 3/4 Cup seasoned bread crumbs
- 1 yellow onion finely chopped (soften in microwave)
- 1/3 Cup chopped garlic
- 1 Tbsp pepper
- 1 Tbsp garlic powder
- 1 Tbsp oregano
- 1 Tbsp onion powder
- 1/2 Cup chopped basil
- 1/2 Cup red wine

1. Combine all meats together then add all remaining ingredients.
2. THEN call everybody that's in your house into your kitchen. No loose hair allowed! (My rule is up in a knot or ponytail)
3. Scrub Hands!
4. Make meatballs according to COOKS WISHES (my friend/chef William Cook says meatballs can be the size of ping pong balls or no bigger than golf balls).
5. Put on cookie sheet.
6. You can fry in hot oil in a pan on the stove or bake in the oven until done.
7. Baptize each meatball in Trilma Leeman's pasta sauce on page 170.

My Mama's Tamale Pie

My Mama's Tamale Pie

- 1 pound ground hamburger or Turkey
- 1 pod garlic chopped
- 1 large red onion chopped
- 1 can olives
- 1 can cream corn
- 1 Cup cornmeal
- 3 Tbsp oil
- 1 can Italian stewed tomatoes
- 1/2 Cup evaporated milk

1. Preheat oven to 350 degrees.
2. In an iron skillet, saute' onion and garlic in oil and set aside.
3. Add in meat and cook till brown.
4. Add in all other ingredients.
5. Pour into a seasoned iron skillet and bake at 350 degrees for 35-40 minutes.

Grandquist Goulash

- 1 pound ground sirloin
- 1 package elbow macaroni
- 1 medium onion, chopped
- 1 15 ounce tomato sauce
- 1/3 Cup milk
- 16 ounce package sharp cheddar
- Small Amount of Garlic peeled chopped

1. Preheat oven to 350 degrees.
2. Saute' onion, garlic and meat.
3. Cook macaroni and drain.
4. Pour meat into pan and top with macaroni.
5. Add tomato sauce and milk and combine ingredients together.
6. Bake at 350 degrees for 45 minutes then place cheese on top. Bake another 10-15 minutes.

Momma's Fried Chicken Strips

- 8-10 Boneless & Skinless Breast and thighs (cut the fat off!)
- 6 eggs
- 3/4 Cup cornstarch
- 3 Cups flour
- Oil for frying
- 1 cube melted butter
- 1/2 Cup chopped green onions
- Garlic salt and pepper

1. Cut chicken into pieces or strips.
2. Crack eggs into a bowl and discard egg shells.
3. Prepare flour by mixing flour, cornstarch and add in seasoning, garlic salt and pepper to taste.
4. Dip chicken pieces first in egg then dip in seasoned flour and cornstarch (I put the flour mixture in a ziplock bag) it is easier for coating chicken pieces.
5. Heat oil in pan on medium high heat.
6. Carefully put chicken pieces in pre-heated oil and cook for 5-6 minutes until golden brown, then turn chicken pieces and cook until done or golden brown.
7. Chop ends off of green onions.
8. Add green onions into butter then saute' together until butter is melted (can use the microwave too!)
9. Put butter mixture in small separate bowls for dipping.

Get Ready for the RAVES!

Enchilada Casserole

- 1 Can Cream of Chicken Soup
- 1 Can of Cream of Mushroom Soup
- 1 Chopped Jalapeño Pepper (mild)
- 1 Can Enchilada Sauce (mild)
- 1 Cup Milk
- 1 pound ground sirloin
- 1 Can Chopped Olives
- 1 Dozen Corn Tortillas chopped
- Shredded jack cheese to cover top

1. Preheat oven to 350 degrees.
2. Brown ground sirloin.
3. Heat chicken soup, mushroom soup, jalapeno peppers, enchilada sauce and milk together.
4. Add in chopped olives and tortilla chips.
5. Put all together in a baking dish. Bake at 350 for 45 minutes.
6. Add shredded jack cheese on top and bake for 15 minutes more.

Chicken & Rice with Added Delishes

- 1 stick of butter
- 1 1/2 Cups instant rice
- 1 1/2 Cups water
- 1 can cream of chicken (undiluted)
- 1/2 packet onion soup mix
- Garlic salt, pepper, paprika

1. Preheat oven to 350 degrees.
2. In a large bowl, mix rice, water and soup.
3. Melt the butter in a casserole dish and pour rice mixture over butter.
4. Place cut up chicken pieces on top of rice. Season with garlic salt and pepper and even some paprika!
5. Cover with foil, punch holes in foil and bake at least an hour.
6. Take the foil off the last 10 minutes to "lightly" brown.

Note:

This is the basic recipe. Sometimes I add in vegetables like Broccoli or Spinach or Zucchini. Also Chopped pieces of Hot Links or Smoked sausage. Serve with salad and bread.

Intoxicated Chicken

-This is the recipe of our Sicilian friend William Cook.

- 1/4 Cup olive oil
- 1 cube butter
- 3/4 Cup chopped onion
- 1/3 Cup chopped garlic
- 3 Cups washed and sliced mushrooms
- 8 to 10 chicken pieces breast or thighs
- 1 1/2 Cups chicken broth
- 1 Cup white wine
- 5 tomatoes chopped
- 2 bunches of basil washed (use leaves only)
- Garlic salt and pepper to taste

1. Melt butter in pan and add in olive oil. Stir together.
2. Add in chopped onions, chopped garlic and sliced mushrooms. Saute' together for 10 minutes on medium heat.
3. Add chicken pieces (slather the chicken in butter, olive oil, mushroom mixture).
4. Cook for 7 minutes then add chicken broth and white wine.
5. Let simmer 10 minutes then add chopped tomatoes and fresh basil.
6. Cook down until chicken is tender and sauce has thickened into a glaze.
7. Serve with your choice of pasta.

Pasties (Meat Pies)

-My BFF Suzi Toadvine's Mother, Ellen Henson

My beautiful mother, Ellen Henson, was a Godly, Christian woman who set a wonderful example for my siblings and I as well as the ladies in the churches my father pastored over their years in ministry. She was born in the south and was by all means a proper southern girl! She moved to Detroit, Michigan when the war began so that she could find work. She had already met my father by that time and they were soon to be married. When she married my father, he was a Navy Seaman and he was serving in World War 2 aboard ship. He was home on a brief break and they were married one Sunday night after the evening service was concluded. He left on the ship just a few days later and my mother began working two jobs so that she could save up to go be with my father when he came back to port in a few months. He was stationed at Treasure Island, California. By day, she worked at Briggs Manufacturing as a riveter on the bomb bay doors of the jet bombers. She was one of the famed "riveters" and the pictures we have of her during that time look much like the ones we have seen in advertisements. The sweet little, feminine girl had to wear heavy clothing with steel toed shoes and her long hair tied up on her head. After working grueling, hot days there, she quickly changed her clothes and jumped on a bus to head across town and work the rest of the evening at a small grocery store. When she finished around 10pm, she again took the bus back to her home, only to start it all over the next day.

During this time, she was able to save a considerable amount of money and by the time my father came back to port, she had enough to fly to California and stay with him for 27 days. Can you imagine the planes back in 1944??? I am not sure I would have been so brave! She was amazing!

This recipe comes from the days that she and my father pastored in the Upper Peninsula of Michigan in the city of Escanaba. It was largely an English community and she enjoyed their food. Pasties came to the US from Cornwall, England. Sometimes they are called Cornish pasties or Meat Pies. Pasties have long become a household word since that time as our family loved them! Now my children love them as well. Add a little green salad alongside them and you have a complete dinner. I hope you enjoy them as much as we have!

Suzi Toadvine

Pasties (Meat Pies)

- Pie crust
- 5 large potatoes
- 2 pounds hamburger
- 1 yellow onion
- 1 egg
- Salt and pepper and garlic powder to taste
- 1 stick of butter
- You can add any vegetables that you like as well. Some add carrots, peas, various spices and also either turkey or pork to the mixture. It is just whatever your preference is.

Note: I will typically cut several slits in the top of the crust or if you like, cut your initial in the crust. It will allow the pastie to cook more evenly. If desired, you can brush the top with cream or beaten egg. Repeat until you use all of the dough.
I usually get 6 from this recipe.

1. Preheat oven to 350 degrees.
2. Make your own crust OR you can use Pillsbury ready made crust (you will want 3 packs of 2)
3. Dice the potatoes fairly small so they will cook through.
4. Finely dice the onions and add it to the meat.
5. Add the egg and salt and pepper to taste.
6. Mix everything together well.
7. Lay the crust out flat into a circle and divide the filling into 6 portions.
8. Take 1/6 of the meat mixture and lay it on the right side of the pie crust, completely filling 1/2 of the flat circle. Take 3 Tbsp of butter (cut up) and put on the top of the meat mixture. Do not overfill.
9. Lightly dampen the edges of the crust and carefully fold the remaining dough over the filling and press edges with a fork to seal.
10. You can make them pretty like a pie crust edge if you prefer.
11. Bake at 350 until golden brown, about an hour.
12. Serve with ketchup and store leftovers in the refrigerator.

Enjoy!

Prime Rib

-By Doctor Reverend Steve Allen

- Prime Rib
- Sea salt
- Course pepper

(Mix in bowl coat prime rib)

1. Preheat oven to 500 degrees for 15 minutes, then turn to 275 degrees.
2. Put prime rib in roasting pan.
3. Cook 15 minutes per pound of prime rib
4. Put thermometer in the middle of meat. Meat temp should be 122 to 124 degrees.
5. **Wrap in foil and let meat rest for** 20 minutes. **Use sharp knife to cut into slices.**

Impossible Cheeseburger Pie

-This is the pie that does the impossible by making it's own crust

- 1 pound ground beef
- 1 1/2 cups chopped onion
- 1/2 tsp salt
- 1/4 tsp pepper
- 1 1/2 Cups milk
- 3/4 Cup Bisquick mix
- 3 eggs
- 2 tomatoes, sliced
- 1 Cup shredded cheddar cheese

1. Preheat oven to 400 degrees.
2. Grease 10x1 1/2 inch pie plate.
3. Brown beef and onion, drain. Stir in salt and pepper.
4. Spread in pie plate.
5. Beat milk, baking mix and eggs until smooth. 15 seconds in blender on high or 1 minute with hand beater.
6. Pour into pie plate and bake 25 minutes.
7. Top wth tomatoes, sprinkle with cheese. Bake 5-8 minutes until inserted knife comes out clean.

The Baked Girdle

My mother was very thrifty. Sometimes her clothes dryer took too long to dry the laundry, so she finished drying the clothes in her oven. She would put the oven on barely warm and those garments would come out bone dry. One day she placed her still-damp girdle on the top rack of the oven, turned it on low and went out to work in her splendid rose garden.

The phone began ringing insistently, so she put down her shovel and ran to answer the call. There was an emergency need in the church, they said, and could she please provide one of her famous lasagna dinners.

It seems like mother had a hotline to Heaven, for that very morning she had assembled a pan of her lasagna and put it in the refrigerator. Mom hung up the phone and turned up the oven to 375 degrees to preheat the lasagna. She returned to the garden and worked feverishly to get her roses fertilized and watered.

Considerable time passed outside before her glance was arrested by a cloud of black, billowing smoke pouring through the screen door. She ran into the house and yanked open the oven door to see her JCPenney bargain basement girdle ablaze with fire.

She grabbed a bucket and doused the girdle and the oven with baking soda and dishwater. The kitchen was filled with smoke, but the house was saved. The girdle was not. Needless to say, that was the end of the girdle.

Well, not quite. Mother was a prankster. She sent the charcoaled girdle to my baby girl, Kate, who was attending bible college in Indianapolis, Indiana. Mom loved to tell this story. Every time she told it, we always laughed and loved to tell her how hilarious and clever she was. You will find my mother's lasagna recipe has been upgraded by my girl, Mindy. She revamped her Grandma Jean's recipe and took it to another level by adding zucchini and extra sausage.

Get ready to experience some outrageous lasagna!

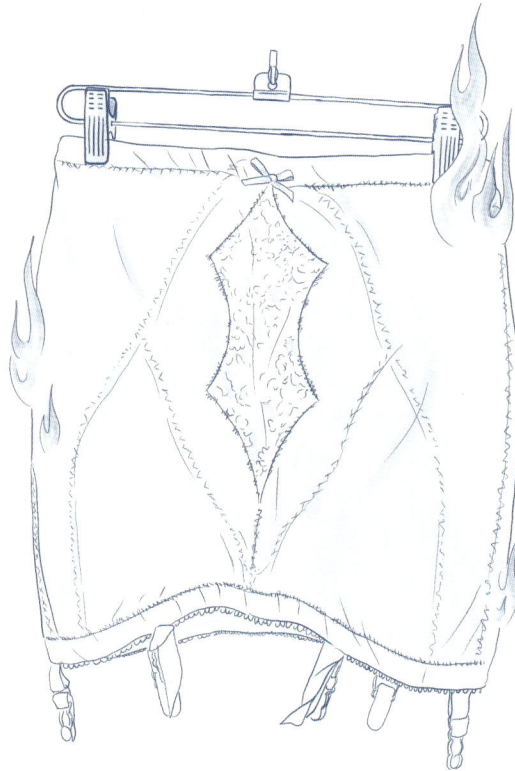

My Mother's Lasagna

-Upgraded by My Mindy Girl. She revamped her Grandma Jean's recipe and took it to another level by adding zucchini and extra sausage.

- 2 Tbsp Cooking Oil
- 1 Clove Garlic, minced
- 1 Medium Onion, chopped
- 1 Pound ground Sirloin
- 2 tsp Salt
- 1/4 tsp Pepper
- 1/2 tsp Oregano
- 1 6 ounce Can Tomato Paste
- 3 Cups Hot Water
- 1/2 Pound Lasagna Noodles, cooked and drained
- 1/2 Pound Ricotta cheese
- Option (1 cup pasta sauce)
- 1/2 Pound Mozzarella Cheese

1. Preheat oven to 350 degrees.
2. In hot oil, fry garlic and onions until soft.
3. Add beef and cook with onion and garlic mixture.
4. Mix in salt and pepper, oregano, tomato paste and blend in water.
5. Simmer for 30 minutes.
6. In a shallow baking dish, pour a layer of sauce, half the noodles, ricotta cheese and thin slices of mozzarella.
7. Bake at 350 until sauce is bubbling. Let stand for 15 minutes before serving. Can also add spinach, zucchini or eggplant between layers.
8. For eggplant: Slice thin and salt both sides of the eggplant pieces.
9. Put on platter, cover and refrigerate for 6 hours.
10. Thoroughly rinse salt from eggplant, pat dry.
11. In a pan, saute eggplant on both sides in 2 Tbsp of butter or olive oil, adding desired garlic salt and pepper. Add to layers of lasagna.

Mindy is probably one of the best cooks of her generation. She is fearless when it comes to cooking dinner for entire school staffs, church functions, and community gathering. She has driven hours to take her delicious meals to discouraged Pastors, sick friends, families dealing with crisis or tragedies.

She has caught my vision, she knows the blessing of pouring out her love from her pots and pans and serving everyone and anyone she can..

I am so proud she is my girl.

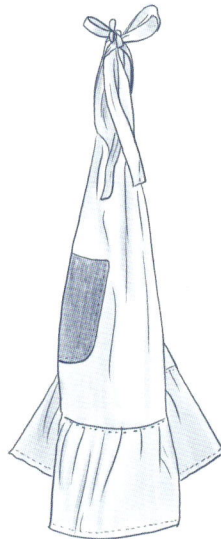

Chooks & Dumplings

-By Doctor Brett Snodgrass

- 2 Cups all purpose flour
- 1 1/2 tsp salt
- Salt and pepper and parsley to taste
- 4 Cups Chicken Broth
- 1 Whole Chicken, Large
- 3/4 Cup milk
- 2 eggs
- 3/4 Cup chopped celery (one inch chunks)
- 3/4 Cup chopped carrots (one inch chunks)
- 3/4 Cup chopped onion (one inch chunks)

1. Fill large pot with 4 cups of chicken broth.
2. Add chopped celery, carrots and onions (for seasoning the broth).
3. Put chicken in pot, cover with water 1/2 inch above chicken and cook on medium.
4. When chicken is thoroughly cooked, put in a colander. Let cool and remove skin and bones. Set chicken meat aside and discard bones and skin.
5. When chicken is cool, shred chicken and set aside.
6. Strain vegetables off broth and set aside.
7. In a bowl, sift flour and salt together.
8. In another bowl, combine eggs and milk, stir.
9. Slowly add egg mixture into flour mixture.
10. After thoroughly mixed, carefully place dumplings into pan of simmering chicken broth.
11. Let cook for 10 minutes on medium high, add in chicken, then cover, lower heat to simmer and cook for 10 more minutes.

Note: Serve with a green salad. You need your greens!

Sister Cox and the Squirrel Tamales

Richard M. and I were invited on a summer day to have dinner at the home of Sister Cox. She was a vision of whiteness. She always wore white flowing dresses with white high heels. Her skin was pure white, bleached by the hot Louisiana sun. Her hair was almost as white as the reflection off of Mt. Rainier on a sunny day. Her mannerisms were ethereal, as the definition of this word would describe her as extremely delicate and light in a way that seems too perfect for this world.

She was a Pentecostal preacher. Although not given to titles, she was known to work in the gifts of prophecy. She was also a good cook and loved to invite folks over to enjoy her savory Louisiana dishes. Back in the day, churches would invite evangelists to come and hold special meetings. These revival services were held seven nights a week, sometimes continuing for several weeks or lasting up to three months—or long enough to convert the whole town to find salvation and be free from the eternal damnation of hellfire and brimstone. The church members were called "saints", and I am convinced these people were made of sturdy stuff to be able to continue raising children, work long, hard hours and make it to church every single night—including two services on Sunday.

Richard M. and I were the evangelists invited to DeRidder, Louisiana by the much-loved and respected Papa George Glass. He was known and revered as the preacher's preacher. We were all gathered around the table enjoying the most wonderful food with our dear friends, Ron and Sherry Liles, and the Glasses, when our hostess delightfully informed us we were eating squirrel tamales. She was proud to tell us that her son was a gifted hunter and had shot them out of the trees in her yard. I almost shot out of my chair.

I really don't remember much after that. I am sure in that moment, however, I learned of the gracing situations that come to us unexpectedly. That lesson has saved us many times, in many places, as we have traveled the world and been the honored invited guests to eat things that were unidentifiable and sometimes unknowable. When we are asked to offer grace, we bow our hearts and offer a word of thanksgiving for the food we are about to eat with the most sincere prayers.

In these moments of not knowing exactly what it is that we are eating, God has been so good to give us grace to eat and be thankful. He helps us to be glad for the happy expressions on the faces of our hosts and those who labored to give us a feast from their fields and other sources. There has never been any doubt of the love and generosity given from the hearts of those who give their best to celebrate us and our coming to visit and share the love of Jesus Christ. We have been infinitely blessed.

Priscilla's Authentic Tamale Feast

-This recipe is to feed a crowd and can be cut down for a smaller crowd. Depending on how stuffed you want your tamale to be, medium to large, this recipe can make 7 to 10 dozen tamales.

- 15 pounds of Masa Preparada (prepared dough) Not Masa Harina
- 1 pound of dried chili California or chili Guajillo pods
- 1 pound of dried Pasilla chili pods
- 1 whole white onion, peeled and sliced
- 5 cloves of garlic
- 4 Cups of pork or chicken broth or stock
- Chef Merito Carne or Carne Asada Seasoning
- 1 Tbsp of Cumin
- 3 Tbsp of Dried Oregano
- 3 to 5 Tbsp of butter
- Salt to taste
- 15 pounds of Pork Butt or Shoulder OR 15 pounds of Country Pork Ribs
- 1/2 pound of Carnitas fat
- 1 to 2 pound of Corn husks
- Water for soaking corn husks

Priscilla's Authentic Tamale Feast Cont.

Husk:

1. Place the dry corn husks in a large bowl or sink of very warm water, and submerge the corn husks.
2. Weigh the husks down and let soak for 1-2 hours or until pliable.
3. Rinse each husk/leaf and drain.

Sauce:

1. Saute onion and garlic in butter until onions are caramelized. Set aside.
2. Cut stems off chilis, cut open and remove seeds.
3. Cut chili into 1-2 inch pieces.
4. Add chopped chilis into a pan large enough to accomodate the 2 pounds of dried chilis, and toast.
5. Toss frequently so not to burn.
6. Add onion mixture to toasted chilis and add enough broth or stock to cover the chilis and onions.
7. Simmer until chili pods are soft.
8. When soft, pour into blender and blend until smooth.
9. May need to be done in two batches. Add more broth as needed and blend to a thick gravy consistency.
10. Caution: Mixture is HOT! Remove the cup inside the lid of the blender, cover lid with paper towel and blend. This allows the heat to disperse and you will not get a pressure splatter from your blender when you take the lid off.

Priscilla's Authentic Tamale Feast Cont.

Masa:

In large bowl put masa and add in 3/4 to 1 Cup of chili sauce. Add 1/2 to 3/4 Cup of pork fat and 2 tsp of salt. Mix well.

The goal is to achieve:

1. A smooth, spreadable texture.
2. Good flavor, taste the mix.
3. Nice color, it should have a reddish hue and adding sauce gives the masa a savory flavor.

Pork:

1. Prepare meat (bake, sauté, hot pot or pressure cooker).
 Meat should be well seasoned, tender. Be careful not to overcook meat, this can cause it to be dry or stringy.
2. When meat is finished cooking, add in chili sauce, cumin, and oregano.
Put enough sauce to cover the meat until thoroughly coated being careful that it is not too wet.
3. Mix well. This is the tamale filling, taste to make sure the seasoning is adequate, if not, add more salt.

Assembling the tamales:

1. Spread masa onto the husk being careful to spread evenly.
2. Fill each tamale husk with 1 to 2 heaping Tbsp of meat filling, wrap tamale.
3. Steam for an hour and serve.

You will know the tamale is done when you peel back the husk, the dough will pull away from the husk.

Priscilla is my friend. I can call her anytime and she will come to see about me. We cook together, and we laugh a lot. We have shared our troubles and found our faith in God to always be enough to carry us through hard times. Someone once told me you can count your true friends on one hand without the use of your thumb. Priscilla is one of those. She is a true and faithful friend and happens to be one of the best tamale makers in all the land.

Nannybones Roast Beast

Nannybones Roast Beast

- 1 1/2 Cup red wine
- 1/3 Cup chopped garlic
- 1/3 Cup olive oil
- 1 1/2 Tbsp garlic salt
- 1 1/2 Tbsp Lipton onion soup mix
- 1 Roast

1. Preheat oven to 300 or 325 degrees.
2. Put roast in zip lock bag and marinate with all ingredients for 24 hours.
3. To bake, oven should be between 300-325 degrees and cook for 4 to 5 hours (for bigger roast, bake accordingly).
4. Put in pan and cover with foil. Cut holes in foil and cook according to poundage.
5. Last hour of cooking uncover so roast will crust on edges and top.

Note: You can also use a crockpot. Put roast in crockpot and cook for 6 to 7 hours. Many times I have put on a big roast and let in cook through the night. Waking up to the smell of that roast is wonderful!

It's like my fairy godmother came in the night and cooked our dinner! Get ready for the ROAR of HAPPINESS when you serve this to your people!

Richard the Third Rocks the Tomahawk Rib-Eye

- 2 Large Tomahawk steaks
- 2 Tbsp kosher salt
- 2 Tbsp ground black pepper
- 1 Tbsp paprika
- 1/2 Tbsp garlic powder
- 1/2 Tbsp onion powder
- 1/2 Tbsp brown sugar
- 1 tsp ground mustard
- 1/4 tsp cayenne pepper
- 1 tsp kitchen crack

1. In a small bowl, combine all ingredients for the rub.
2. Season the steaks liberally with the rub and set steaks aside while the grill preheats.
3. Meat should be room temperature.
4. While cooking, melt butter then drip on ribeye and add some thyme and rosemary flakes. (optional)
5. Use smoker if possible. Set temperature of grill at 225 degrees, preheat for 15 minutes.
6. Cook until desired taste.

It doesn't get better than a massive tomahawk steak on a Traeger grill. Smoke these ribeyes for up to an hour, or until their internal temp reaches 120°F. Then crank up the heat, sear both sides, and serve up some beefy wood-fired flavor.

Tallerine Casserole

-By Donna Frost

- 1 1/2 pounds ground beef
- 1 medium onion, chopped
- 1 can (10 3/4 oz) tomato soup
- 1/2 Cup ketchup
- 1 Cup water
- 1 can (6 oz) pitted, ripe olives
- 1 tsp salt
- 1 can (1 lb.) whole kernel corn
- 1 pkg 8oz egg noodles
- 1 Cup grated American cheese

1. Preheat oven to 350 degrees.
2. Crumble meat into skillet and cook over moderate heat until it loses red color.
3. Add onion during last five minutes cooking time and drain off grease.
4. Combine soup, ketchup, water and juice from olives and add to meat.
5. Cut olives in half, reserve a few whole olives to garnish top of casserole.
6. Add olive halves, salt and corn to meat mixture.
7. Use about one-half package of the noodles. Break noodles in pieces, add to meat.
8. Bake, covered, in 350 degree oven for about 45 minutes or until noodles are done.
9. Stir occasionally during baking.
10. Sprinkle cheese on top and garnish with whole olives.
11. Return to oven just until cheese melts.

St. Jean Sour Cream Chicken Enchiladas

-My mama's recipe

- 1 Onion chopped
- 1 Garlic clove, crushed
- 1 cube Butter
- 4 Cups shredded cheese (your choice)
- 1 small can Chopped green chilis
- 1 Chicken skinned and deboned
- 1 Cup Sour cream
- 1 large can Cream of Chicken soup
- Corn tortillas
- Garlic salt and pepper
- Lipton onion soup mix

1. Preheat oven to 375 degrees.
2. Season chicken with garlic salt, wrap chicken in foil and bake on 375 degrees for 1 hour.
3. In a large pan, melt butter.
4. Add chopped onion, crushed or minced garlic, green chili mixture and season with garlic salt and pepper, and stir.
5. When chicken is done, pour off chicken broth into the onion, garlic, green chili mixture.
6. Season with garlic salt and pepper and stir.
7. Shred chicken.
8. Add chicken soup and sour cream then add in the shredded chicken, mix gently. Reserve a few Tbsp chicken soup for later.
9. Warm the corn tortillas (I put them in some warm chicken broth while preparing the chicken).
10. Fill the tortillas with the chicken mix and add some shredded cheese of your choice. I use jack or mozzarella!
11. Put a few tablespoons of cream of chicken soup in bottom of baking pan.
12. Roll each enchilada and put in pan. Put cheese on top of enchiladas and cover with foil.
13. Bake on 350 for 25 minutes.
14. Remove foil and cook for 5-10 minutes.

Veggies

"God will carry you through the storm".

Isaiah 43:2

Roasted Whole Baby Pumpkins

-Chef Dave Vartanian gifted this Baby Pumpkin Recipe 25 years ago. Visit his restaurant "Vintage Press" in Visalia, California for fine dining.

- 6 Baby Pumpkins
- 4 ounces Jarlsburg Cheese
- 8 ounces smoked chicken, diced
- 2 Tbsp hot chili sauce
- 1 onion, chopped
- 1 Tbsp butter
- 6 ounces heavy cream
- 1 Tbsp chives
- salt and pepper to taste
- Lemon Butter Sauce, Page 166

1. Preheat oven to 325 degrees.
2. Place pumpkins whole into a baking pan, cover with foil and bake for 45 minutes or until the pumpkins are soft.
3. Using a sharp knife, remove the tops of the pumpkins, discard the seeds and season the inside with salt and pepper.
4. Heat the butter in a saute pan and cook the onion over medium heat until soft.
5. In a bowl, combine the smoked chicken, Jarlsburg cheese, cooked onion and chives. Mix well and then season with salt, pepper and chili sauce to taste.
6. Fill the pumpkins with the smoked chicken mixture and pour one ounce of heavy cream into each pumpkin.
7. Place the tops back onto each pumpkin, cover with aluminum foil and roast the pumpkins in a 350 degree oven for 15-2o minutes.
8. To serve, place one ounce of lemon butter sauce on each of six warm plates and place a pumpkin on each plate. Serves 6 as a first course.

Nannybones Corn Pudding

- 3 Cups fresh or frozen corn (I prefer petite white corn)
- 3 eggs
- 1 1/2 tsp sugar
- 1 Cup cream
- 1 1/2 tsp salt and pepper
- 1 stick melted butter

1. Preheat oven to 325 degrees.
2. Mix all ingredients together in a large bowl and place in buttered dish.
3. Cook for 45 minutes until golden brown.

Southern Creamed Corn

- 4 Corn on the cob
- Water
- Salt to taste
- 1 Tbsp butter
- 1 to 2 Tbsp bacon grease

White Sauce:
- 3/4 Cup milk
- 1 Tbsp flour

1. Cut corn off cob and put into skillet.
2. Add water, enough to cover corn.
3. Add salt and bacon grease and cook for 5-10 minutes, then add white sauce.
4. To make white sauce, in a small bowl, combine milk and add flour and stir well. Simmer.

My Green Beans

- 6 cans green beans, drained
- 6 pieces bacon, cut into pieces
- 1 large yellow or white onion, chopped
- Garlic salt and Garlic pepper to taste
- 1 Tbsp Dry onion soup mix
- 1/2 cube butter

1. In a large pot, melt butter, then add onions and bacon.
2. Cook until onions are translucent and bacon is cooked through.
3. Add in green beans, salt and pepper and dry onion soup mix.
4. Make sure you thoroughly coat the green beans with seasonings.

Note: Sometimes I add mushrooms, hot links or sausage.

Veggie Pie

- 2 deep dish pie crust (store bought or homemade)
- 1 yellow onion , chopped
- 1 bell pepper, chopped
- 4 squash
- 4 tomatoes
- 1/2 jar Green Giant mushrooms
- 1 stick of butter
- Garlic salt and pepper
- 2 Cups Mozzarella cheese
- 1/2 Cup mayonnaise

1. Preheat oven to 350 degrees.
2. Saute onions and bell pepper in butter.
3. Place into crust: 2 thin layers of sliced yellow squash, 2 layers peeled and sliced fresh tomatoes, cover with 1/2 jar Green Giant mushrooms.
4. Divide saute mixture between pies and add saute mix on top of vegetables.
5. Salt and pepper to taste.
6. Mix mozzarella cheese with mayonnaise and apply this mixture to the top of pie, like a meringue!
7. Bake for 1 hour or until golden brown.

Green Bean Casserole

-My Gram's Favorite

- 4 bags frozen French cut green beans
- 1 Can mushroom soup
- 1 Can asparagus soup
- 1 to 2 jars bacon cheese spread
- 1 Can water chestnuts (drained)
- 1 Can French fried onion rings
- Garlic salt and pepper

1. Preheat oven to 350 degrees.
2. In a bowl, combine green beans with mushroom and asparagus soups, do not add water.
3. Soften bacon cheese spread then distribute over bean mixture.
4. Gently fold water chestnuts into green bean mixture.
5. Salt & Pepper to taste.
6. Put in a baking dish and bake at 350 degrees for 20 minutes.
7. Sprinkle dried onion rings over top of the green beans.
8. Let onion rings bake until golden brown, about 5-7 minutes.

Although there are many diverse green bean recipes, my Heidi thinks nothing can touch this tried and true Green Bean Casserole.

Summer Zucchini

- 1 very large zucchini
- 2 Cups instant rice
- 2 Cups mushrooms washed, chopped
- 1 large yellow onion peeled, chopped
- 2 cloves Garlic peeled, chopped
- 1 can cream of chicken soup
- 2 Tbsp Worcestershire sauce
- 1/3 Cup olive oil
- 1/2 stick of butter
- Ground turkey or hamburger meat
- Dry Lipton Onion soup mix

1. Preheat oven to 375 degrees.
2. Wash zucchini, cut in half lengthwise and scoop out the seeds and discard. Cut out the meat of the zucchini and chop into small pieces.
3. Cook rice until almost done (set aside until cool).
4. In a pan, add olive oil and butter. Saute' onions and garlic, add mushrooms and Worcestershire sauce and cook for 6 or 7 minutes, add in turkey meat and zucchini.
5. Season with Lipton onion soup mix and add garlic and pepper.
6. Mix all ingredients together then add cream of chicken soup (sometimes I make it without cream of chicken soup). Fill the zucchini to overflowing with rice mixture.
7. Wrap zucchini in foil and bake at 375 degrees for 45 minutes

This is a Summer "Must!"

Picnics at Bodega Bay

Bodega Bay with its beautiful, flawless rocky beaches was our second home. It became part of our family traditions to celebrate birthdays and holidays—and whatever excuse we could find to spend time together on those beautiful, unblemished beaches. We gathered driftwood and built fires to heat up cans of pork and beans and roast hot dogs and marshmallows. It was simple and so much fun.

Forever imprinted to my memory is our Viking dad who taught David and me how to bodysurf on those beaches. In my mind's eye, I can still see the tall, vivid silhouette of my father shouting above the roar of the crashing waves, "THROW YOURSELF INTO THE WAVE!! DON'T BE AFRAID!! IT WILL BRING YOU BACK IN!!"

We cared not that the Pacific Ocean water was so frigid that it turned our lips blue and took away our breath when we dove in, or that the great white sharks shared those same waters. We never gave it a second thought! Looking back and remembering those magical days in my life, I understand how important it is for us to take the time and make memories with the people we love. Life is fleeting, so we must be intentional about the way we spend our days. We only get this one chance. Let's do it big!

Big Time Barbecued Baked Beans

- 3-12 ounce cans Baked Beans (Bush is my fave)
- 1 large yellow onion, finely chopped
- 1 1/4 Cup brown sugar
- 3/4 Cup ketchup
- 1/4 Cup mustard
- 1/2 Cup Sweet Baby Rays Barbecue Sauce (sometimes I add more)
- 1/4 Cup maple syrup
- 4-6 hot links chopped in pieces
- 6-8 pieces bacon cut in 2 inch strips

1. Preheat oven to 350 degrees.
2. Put baked beans in a large bowl.
3. Add in chopped onions, mixing them in well and then add all remaining ingredients except bacon.
4. Pour baked bean mixture into glass or metal pan.
5. Place bacon piece on top.
6. Bake at 350 degrees for 50 minutes or until bacon is done completely.
7. Top of baked beans should have a glazed look when done.

They will ask for seconds
They will ask for thirds.
They will skip potato chips
They will skip desserts!
And They will say,
"MORE BAKED BEANS PLEASE!"
I can HEAR THEM ROAR:
"All Hail to The Baked Bean King"
OR
"All Hail to The Baked Bean Queen".

Maple Roasted Brussels Sprouts & Butternut Squash

-By Heidi King

- 1 pound brussels sprouts (ends trimmed, sliced in half)
- 1 pound butternut squash peeled, seeded, and cubed
- 6 bacon strips
- 3 Tbsp olive oil
- 4 Tbsp real maple syrup divided
- Salt and pepper
- 1 tsp kitchen crack
- 1 Cup whole pecans
- 1/2 Cup dried cranberries

1. Preheat oven to 425 degrees.
2. Line a baking sheet with aluminum foil and spray with non stick spray.
3. In a large bowl, combine brussels spouts, butternut squash, and olive oil. Toss with olive oil and 1 Tbsp maple syrup. Salt and pepper, add kitchen crack.
4. Spread evenly on the baking sheet. Slice the bacon strips and lay them on top of the Brussels Sprouts and Butternut squash pieces (scatter bacon evenly). Roast in the oven for 20 to 30 minutes until the sprouts and squash are done and the bacon is crisp.
5. Remove from the oven and put roasted sprouts and squash back into the large bowl.
6. Add pecans, cranberries and remaining maple syrup and toss for extra delish! Enjoy!

The People will cheer your name!

My Gram's Fried Green Tomatoes

- 2/3 Cup instant flour such as Wondra, divided
- 1 1/2 tsp kosher salt
- 3/4 tsp paprika
- 3/4 Cup buttermilk
- 1 large egg white
- 1 1/2 tsp hot sauce, such as Louisiana or Tabasco
- 3/4 Cup finely ground cornmeal
- 3 unripe green tomatoes (about 1 1/2 pounds total), cut into 1/4-inch thick slices
- 1/2 Cup canola oil
- Option: Parmesan cheese

1. In a shallow dish, whisk together 1/3 cup flour, salt and paprika.
2. In a separate shallow dish, whisk together the buttermilk, egg white and hot sauce.
3. In a third shallow dish, stir together the cornmeal and remaining 1/3 cup flour.
4. Next, place a wire rack in a rimmed baking sheet.
5. Prepare the tomatoes by dipping each slice in the flour, buttermilk and then cornmeal.
6. Place the breaded slices on the wire rack in a single layer.
7. Over medium-high heat, heat the oil in a large cast-iron skillet.
8. Carefully fry the tomatoes in batches until golden-brown (3-5 minutes per side) transfer to a paper towel-lined plate. Repeat until you've fried all the tomatoes.
9. If desired, sprinkle the hot tomatoes with parmesan cheese before serving.

Poppy's Smokehouse Butter Beans

- 2 pounds dry baby Lima beans
- 1 medium chopped onion
- 1 pound bacon cut into I inch pieces
- 1 rounded Tbsp of chicken Bouillion
- 1/2 tsp salt
- 1/4 tsp black pepper
- 1/2 tsp garlic salt

1. Put beans in a pot (use smoker if available) cover and soak for 2 hours.
2. In pan, fry bacon until crisp.
3. Drain beans in colander then put back into pot, add the fried bacon and all other ingredients.
4. Cover the beans with up to 1 or 2 inches of water, bring to a boil then turn down heat to medium-low.
5. Simmer for 2-3 hours or until beans are tender.

Zucchini & Sausage Dish

-Gomes guys' favorite

- 2-3 pounds organic Zucchini
- 1/2 pound hot Italian sausage
- 1/4 Cup virgin olive oil
- 2-3 Tbsp of butter
- 2 Tbsp of crushed garlic
- 1 Tbsp garlic salt
- 1 Tbsp garlic pepper
- 2 Tbsp Lipton's dry onion soup mix
- 3/4 Cup yellow onion
- 1/2 Cup fresh basil
- 6 Roma tomatoes
- 3/4 Cup of white wine

1. Wash and prepare zucchini, onion, basil and tomatoes. (I like to cut my zucchini in one inch pieces) but if my grandkids are helping to cut the zucchini I am not particular... It is more about the time together and not perfection of the Zucchini pieces!
2. In pan pour oil and add butter, melt on low heat.. Then add chopped onions, garlic sauté for 7 minutes.
3. Break up sausage in small pieces add to this mixture, cook for 4 minutes.
4. Sprinkle Lipton onion soup mix over ingredients. Cook for 2 minutes, stirring very gently.
5. Then add in zucchini, stir in making sure all zucchini is coated with sauté mixture. After 5 minutes of cooking on medium heat add chopped tomatoes and chopped basil, pour wine over the top of all ingredients, add in garlic salt and pepper
6. Turn heat on low and simmer for 15-20 minutes, being careful to stir the zucchini very gently. Do not over cook zucchini, better if it has some form to it!

Note: Sometimes I add mushrooms to this. Put the mushrooms in when adding the sausage. Serve Sicilian Zucchini as a side dish or you can serve as a stand alone main dish with some garlic bread. This is one of my grandson Josiah's favorite meals.

William Cook taught me how to make this dish... He is one of the best Italian Chefs I know... We have been honored to be friends with William and Joanna for many years... Old friends and Classic Italian cooking is like a fine treasure, a pot of priceless gold

Sweet Potato & Yam Hash

- 2 large sweet potatoes
- 2 large yams
- 2-4 Jalapeños
- 1 large sweet onion
- 1 pound of bacon
- Olive oil
- Salt and Pepper to taste

1. Clean potatoes and yams and rub with olive oil.
2. Put on baking sheet and bake at 400 degrees for 30-45 minutes (should be able to pierce with a fork with light pressure. **DO NOT** fully cook!)
3. **Chop** onions, cut potatoes into cubes, **slice** or chop jalapenos.
4. **Cut** bacon into small pieces and cook **down** until crisp. Remove from pan.
5. **R**eserving bacon grease in skillet, add in **o**nions, jalapenos and potatoes.
6. Allow potato mixture to cook until crisp on one side, stir or toss and cook until crisp on the other side!
7. You can sprinkle bacon bits on hash, or skip it.

Note: If you want to make this a vegetarian **dish**, then cook with olive oil and leave out the **bacon!**

Succotash for Summer Days

- 4 pieces Bacon
- 1 yellow onion chopped
- 2 garlic cloves peeled and chopped
- 3 Cups fresh or frozen lima beans
- 3 Cups fresh or frozen corn
- 2 ripe tomatoes peeled and chopped
- 2 Tbsp butter
- Salt and pepper and fresh herbs

1. In a pan, fry bacon until crisp.
2. Drain bacon pieces on paper towel.
3. In left over bacon grease, melt butter then add in onion and garlic. Saute' until soft but not overcooked.
4. Add in vegetables and cook for 10 minutes on medium to medium low temperature.
5. Salt and pepper to taste.
6. Cover with lid and simmer on lowest setting for 10 minutes.

Serving suggestions:

This makes a wonderful side dish with pork chops or fried catfish. Succotash can even dress-up a hamburger patty. This is one of my faves. This dish has enough integrity that it can stand alone on its finer merits of homemade delish.

Kate Ashley's 5 Star Golden Mashed Potatoes

- 10 gold Yukon potatoes (Can use red potatoes)
- 1 stick butter (melted)
- 1/2 to 2/3 Cup liquid heavy cream (warm in microwave)
- Salt and pepper to taste

1. Wash and prepare potatoes.
2. Your choice to peel or not to peel, that is the question!
3. Cut potatoes into one inch pieces and put into a large pot, fill with water that covers potatoes. Your preference to add salt into the water.
4. Boil potatoes on medium-high for 15 minutes or until soft. Test with a fork.
5. Carefully drain off the water (I like to save potato liquid because it makes a good base for soup! Let it cool and then store in freezer ziplock bags, lay flat in the freezer)
6. Pour melted butter and warm heavy cream into potatoes.
7. Mash or whip the potatoes until creamy. Be careful to not over whip the potatoes.
8. To serve, place potatoes in a bowl and garnish with a bit of butter.

The first time I ate Kate's mashed potatoes I could not believe the layers of flavor. The honest to goodness taste of those potatoes could allow for them to rule and reign over all other vegetable offerings. You do take a chance of never being satisfied with any other potato dishes after tasting just one extraordinary spoonful of my beautiful baby girl's perfect version of mashed potatoes. She says it's in the love for the ones she is cooking for that makes them so delicious. I believe her.

Best Beet Salad

- 2-3 Large Beets or (4 to 5 small beets)
- Olive oil
- Salt and Pepper
- 2 Cups Arugula (washed and dried)
- 2-4 ounces Gorgonzola, Blue or Goat cheese crumbled
- Balsamic glaze
- Candied Pecans or Walnuts

1. Preheat oven to 350-400 degrees.
2. Trim off greens from beets and wash thoroughly.
3. Place beets in a large square of foil.
4. Drizzle with olive oil and salt and pepper.
5. Close up foil to make a pouch.
6. Bake in 350-400 degree oven for 30-45 minutes until fork tender. Reduce baking time for small beets to 25 minutes.
7. Allow to cool and peel.
8. Slice beets and place arugula on serving plate. Arrange beets on arugula.
9. Drizzle with olive oil and balsamic glaze and sprinkle with cheese crumbles and candied nuts over beets.

Not all cheese is created equal.
Blue cheese is high in sodium and calories.
Parmesan, Part-skim Mozzarella, Camembert, Swiss cheese and Cottage cheese are considered lower in calorie.
Feta is also a good choice if counting calories.
A strong but vibrant taste is found in Goat cheese and Gorgonzola. Cheese goes back to the ancient days, so anything that has been around that long deserves a place on our table. We eat sharp 15 year aged cheese on crackers for Breakfast, it is a quiet storm of delish to start out our day.
We love it!

Charcuterie

"You shall eat in plenty and be satisfied, and praise the name of the Lord your God, who has dealt wondrously with you."

Joel 2:26

Honey Pecan Baked Brie Board

- 1 Brie wheel
- 1/4 Cup of Honey
- 1/2 Cup of chopped Pecans
- Rosemary & Sage garnish
- Sliced Baguette
- Strawberries
- Blackberries
- Raspberries
- Ranier Cherries
- Dried fig
- Candied oranges

1. Preheat oven to 350 degrees.
2. Remove Brie wheel from packaging, leave the Brie rind on.
3. Place Brie into a small cast iron skillet. If you do not own a cast iron skillet, you can use any baking dish.
4. Bake Brie for 10-15 minutes.
5. While Brie is in oven, combine the honey and chopped pecans into a small bowl and mix together.
6. Once Brie is baked, remove from oven and cut a small wedge of of the wheel to allow the cheese to start flowing!
7. Pour honey and pecan mixture over the Brie.

Serve with sliced baguette and fruit

Movie Night Board

- Popcorn
- Milk Duds
- Sour Patch kids
- Pull & peel Twizzlers
- Mini peanut butter cups
- M&M's
- Yogurt-covered Pretzels
- Swedish Fish
- Rattle snake gummies
- Peach gummy rings
- Mike & Ike
- Sour bears
- 3 ramekins

1. Select your favorite movie snacks.
2. Place popcorn top right.
3. Fill ramekins with Milk Duds, jelly beans and M&M's.
4. Place your favorite candy in bunches.

Honey Pecan Baked Brie Board

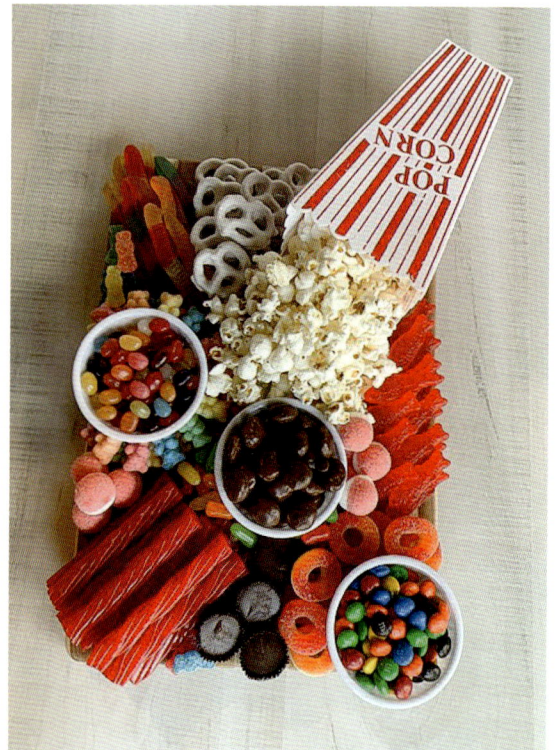

Movie Night Board

Kids Board

- Peanut butter jelly sandwich cut in triangles
- Ramekin bowl for goldfish
- Rice Krispy squares
- Rainbow carrots
- Celery
- Beef sticks
- Turkey deli meat
- Cubed Colby
- Babybel
- Apple slices
- Strawberries cut in halves
- Grapes
- Blackberries
- Blueberries
- Yogurt covered pretzels

1. Place triangle peanut butter sandwiches across your board.
2. Fill ramekin bowl with Goldfish, place top right on the board.
3. Cut rice Krispy squares and place them around goldfish ramekin.
4. Unwrap Babybel cheese leaving the wax on. Use any cookie cutter to pierce out through the wax and get desired shape. Place Babybel top center of your board.
5. Cube Colby cheese, place top left under peanut butter sandwiches.
6. Slice rainbow carrots and celery in halves. Place them bottom right at the end of the sandwiches.
7. Roll turkey slices and wedge in between rice Krispy squares and sandwiches.
8. Cut beef sticks next to Colby cheese.
9. Place all fruit bunch of grapes, fan sliced apples, strawberry halves, blueberries and blackberries.
10. Place yogurt covered pretzels across Babybel.

Serve with juice box \or milk

S'more Board

- S'mores heat fuel can
- Graham crackers
- Butter waffle cookie
- Marshmallow regular & mini size
- Milk chocolate & cookies & cream squares
- Reese's peanut butter cups
- Hazelnut spread
- Peanut Butter
- Honey
- Strawberries
- Blackberries
- Chocolate truffle
- 3 bowls

1. Place heat can in the middle of your board.
2. Fill bowls with honey, peanut butter and hazelnut spread. Place bowls on opposite ends of board.
3. Stagger Graham crackers and butter waffle cookies.
4. Stagger milk chocolate and cookies & cream chocolate.
5. Fan out Reese's peanut butter cups.
6. Place strawberry halves around hazelnut spread.
7. Fill the rest of the board with regular and mini marshmallows.
8. Place chocolate truffle & blackberries.

Enjoy all the different combinations!

Kids Board

S'mores Board

Caprese Skewer

- Mini tomato medley
- Ciliegine Fresh Mozzarella
- Fresh Basil
- Cracked pepper
- Dried oregano
- Balsamic glaze
- Baguette bread
- Skewers
- Fresh sage for garnish
- Ramekin

1. Fill ramekin with balsamic glaze, place in the middle of your board.
2. Skewer a tomato, piece of basil, a mozzarella ball and another tomato. Repeat to fill board.
3. Place skewers side by side on board.
4. Fill gaps in with baguette bread.
5. Sprinkle oregano and cracked pepper over skewers.

Cheese Board

- 5 types of cheese, hard to soft Manchego (sheep cheese), Gouda, English Stilton (Blue cheese), Brie wedge (cow cheese), Cranberry goat cheese.
- 2 types of meat Italian dry salami and Prosciutto
- Strawberries, grapes, blackberries, raspberries, blueberries and Rainier cherries.
- Fig butter
- Cornichon and olives
- Honey
- A variety of crackers
- Praline pecans and Marcona almonds
- Yogurt covered pretzels & dark chocolate squares
- Dried oranges & figs
- Rosemary & Sage for garnish

1. Fill ramekins with Fig butter, honey and cornichon and olives. Place on board.
2. Place your cheeses.
3. Place your meats.
4. Fan out your crackers on the edge of your board.
5. Place your fruit.
6. Fill in gaps with nuts.
7. Layer yogurt covered pretzels and chocolate squares.
8. Place dried oranges and figs.
9. Place garnish.

Caprese Skewer

Cheese Board

Special Thanks to:

Brian & Jessica Sublet
Graze A Board LLC
www.grazeaboard.com

@grazeaboard

DRINKS

"We must keep our eyes on Jesus, who leads us, and makes
our faith complete".
Hebrews 12:2

Simple Punch

- 3 Quarts Ginger Ale
- 1/2 Gallon Lime Sherbet

1. Put sherbet in large container
2. Gently pour ginger ale over the sherbet.
3. Serve.

Spice Tea

- 2 Cups Tang
- 1 Cup Instant Tea
- 1 1/2 Cups sugar
- 1 package Lemon Twist
- 2 tsp ground cloves

1. Mix all ingredients.
2. Store in an airtight jar.

Cranberry Banana Punch

- 1/2 pound fresh or frozen cranberries
- 3 Cups of sugar
- 6 Cups of water
- 1 large can frozen lemonade
- 5 bananas
- 46 ounces pineapple juice
- 1 block of dry ice

1. Place cranberries in pot of water, add just enough water to cook berries until they pop open.
2. Strain juice and add frozen lemonade, sugar, water and bananas and blend.
3. Pour into a large container and add pineapple juice.
4. Divide into 3 equal parts and freeze for at least 4 hours.
5. Pour 3 quarts (1 per portion) over block of dry ice, mix slushy.

Strawberry Slush

- 7 Cups of water
- 4 Cups of sugar
- 1 large banana/strawberry jello
- 1 large can of frozen orange juice
- 1 can crushed pineapple
- 2 packages frozen strawberries, crushed
- 1 lemon rind
- 1 liter 7-up

1. Boil water and sugar together.
2. Add jello to hot mixture.
3. Add orange juice, pineapple, strawberries and lemon rind.
4. Let freeze for 24 hours.
5. Let stand at room temperature.
6. Pour 7-up over mixture then put in glasses and serve.

Egg Nog

- 3 half pints of whipping cream
- 2 cans Eagle Brand Milk
- 3 pints milk
- 1 1/2 tsp vanilla flavor
- 2 tsp nutmeg

1. Whip cream and put in refrigerator.
2. Mix Eagle Brand milk, 3 pints of milk, vanilla flavor and nutmeg.
3. Fold in whipped cream.
4. Chill in freezer till thick.

Note: Sugar is optional.

One Very Small Act

Oh, Gram. You've been gone so long. It's been at least 27 years. There are so many lessons you taught me, and I didn't even realize they were lessons or that you were teaching me. My brother, David, and I thought we were the luckiest kids in the world to have such a smart, sweet Gram. You smelled exactly like your garden of roses. We had no idea that people looking in on our story might perceive you as poor and uneducated. You were simply the best. Too wonderful for words.

Once I brought a friend with me to meet Gram. She didn't have a grandmother, so I thought she should meet a true and perfect one. She loved Gram, and was in awe of the gentle kindness extended to her.

My friend had a terribly infected sore on her foot. It looked like it could turn gangrenous any second. I remember Gram rummaging around in her kitchen cabinet until she found a suitable pan. She filled it with warm water and added a cup of Epsom salts. She encouraged my friend to soak her foot as long as she could and helped her commit to that soaking by making her famous eggnog. That eggnog was a sure cure for whatever body part or ailing soul might be hurting. As I stir up the memory of that eggnog, I recollect it was pretty heavy on the milk and cream, raw eggs, a ton of sugar and a liberal splash of vanilla.

Nowadays we hear warnings of the dangers of consuming raw eggs, but Lord knows I must have had several near-death experiences back then from consuming Gram's organic eggnog and other life-threatening snacks and drinks she loved to serve us. After an hour or so in the Epsom salts water, my friend's foot was thoroughly soaked and distinctively shriveled. We laughed and commented how it looked a lot like a long-forgotten, leftover Gravenstein apple from the bottom of Gram's icebox.

Gram put my friend's foot in a fresh white towel that she had just taken off the clothesline. The towel smelled like a breath of fresh heaven. She held that little foot in her lap as she ripped up an old sheet into strips. She carefully doctored the wound with ointment, then skillfully wrapped the foot in those white clean strips. Then she found one of my Granddad's white socks. (The other sock had gone on to who knows where in that great sock heaven in the sky). Gram slipped that white sock over the well-dressed foot, then with a gentle pat on my friend's knee, said, "Now honey, I've done all I can to help your foot heal, but you have to stay out of the dirt and keep it clean."

It was such a simple act of kindness. It was the very essence of goodness. It was care and concern for an orphaned child, obviously without a mother or dad to see about her little foot. But Gram knew. She could sense this little girl needed to know how precious and important she was.

Gram was wise. She taught me the importance of taking care of the small things. My friend's infected foot may have seemed insignificant, but it could have become very serious if not tended.

Gram taught me to care about the marginalized and the discarded, the broken and lost ones of our world. None of these are ever insignificant. Their trouble and heartache may not appear to be the collapse of the whole world, but it could be their whole world coming apart at the seams.

We never know the magic our love can bring through one small act of caring. Just one very small act. It can change someone's world forever.

Granmommie's Milkshake

- 1 egg
- 1 banana
- 1 tsp honey
- 1/2 Cup of milk
- 3/4 Cup of vanilla ice cream

1. Beat egg first.
2. Add banana and honey to beaten egg.
3. Beat again and add milk.
4. Beat again and add ice cream, do not beat.

Drink up!

Citrus Punch

- 64 oz pineapple juice
- 64 oz apricot nectar
- 8 oz frozen orange juice
- 8 oz frozen lemonade
- 1 bottle Grenadine
- 2 liters 7-up

1. In a large bowl, combine all juices.
2. Once combined, stir in Grenadine syrup.
3. Add 7-up to bowl and serve

Party on!

Fancy Nancy

- 1 chilled bottle or can 7-up
- 1 to 2 Tbsp Grenadine syrup
- 1/2 Cup of orange juice
- Slice of lime or strawberry
- Glass of ice

1. Fill glass 3/4 full of 7-up and add syrup and orange juice and stir well.
2. Add ice and garnish the top edge of glass with lime, orange or strawberry slices.

Note: Sometimes I dip the top of glasses in water and then dredge them by putting the rim into a shallow plate of sugar, then put glasses in freezer. When ready to serve this delicious drink, carefully take the glasses out of freezer and place on a serving tray. Then make the drink as I have suggested.

They don't call me "Fancy Nancy" for nothin!

Celebration on the Rocks

- 2 bags of dry ice
- 2 liters coke-a-cola or 2 bottles of Sparkling Cider

1. In a large bowl, add dry ice.
2. DO NOT touch dry ice with hands, use pot holders.
3. When everyone is gathered around the bowl, pour coke (or Cider) over dry ice!

It will erupt into a cloud of glorious shock and awe. Ladle coke into glasses, being careful not to break apart the dry ice (let it dissolve organically). Even grown-ups will be caught-up in the moment of such a fun celebration drink!

celebration on the rocks

The Toast

David, Tracy and their six beautiful children all lived on the same acre of land in Santa Rosa where my parents lived for years. Their houses are just a yard apart from each other. David and Tracy's children were all conceived and born in that house with its two tiny bedrooms. My brother always said that two bedrooms were more than enough. He and Tracy never seemed bothered by the fact that there were eight people living in the house.

David was an inventor of sorts—a creator. He was an absolute master on the guitar and harmonica and he composed incredible songs about the Lord, his family, and the blessings of knowing God. He also built a huge pond on the property, complete with waterfalls, beautiful plants and halogen lights (which he put in old Mason glass jars so that the lights actually looked like the fireflies we used to catch in the summertime as kids).

One particular morning, I got up early and went to sit by his pond. Everywhere I looked I could see my brother's vision, passion and love for life. A little while later, I walked over to his house to see him and found him making the most amazingly wonderful crepes from scratch. I do mean COMPLETELY from scratch, including milling the organic wheat he used for flour. He had also walked outside to the massive blackberry patch that grows on the fence that lines the driveway and picked these huge, fat, ripe blackberries. "Sit down, Nan," he told me, "I'll make you some breakfast."

Although seemingly insignificant, it actually was quite a miracle that it was just the two of us—especially since he had a tribe of eight and I had my tribe of four (plus several grandchildren). As I recall, it was probably the first time since we were little that we had spent time alone. Wow. He was a professional crepe maker. I was amazed at his skill and told him so. I remember admitting to him that I had always wanted to learn, but that the crepe thing just looked entirely too fragile for my hands. He responded by laughing and telling me how very simple it was. Then he crushed the berries with his bare hands and looked up at me and said, "I hope you don't mind," (referring to his stained fingers and rough hands).

I reminded him that our Gram (our mother's mother) used to make us fresh strawberries, still warm from the patch, the very same way. David just smiled and served my plate. It was wonderful. The crepes were stuffed full of blackberries and topped with yummy whipped cream that he had added on top in a heart-shaped decoration. I remember feeling amazed when I tasted the hot tea he had prepared. When I asked him what kind it was, he showed me the bag of tea leaves. I was thrilled when I realized that it was my favorite tea—one that I had first experienced in London a few years prior. We were both thrilled to discover that we had been drinking the same tea and had no clue that it was a favorite of both of ours.

Everything in David's house was made from something he had picked up either at the secondhand store, the recycle center, or the dump. He always had a knack for salvaging old, torn up, broken-down castoffs and transforming them into one-of-a-kind originals! We sat that day at one such treasure, the old, beat-up table, talking for hours, lingering over several refills of the delicious hot tea. Then we wrote a new song together.

At some point, we decided to make a toast. David turned to me and asked, "What in the world can we toast to?" Both of us sat in silence for a few seconds. While we immensely enjoyed each other's company, we felt the intense sorrow that came with knowing it would be just a few short weeks until his final departure from this earth.

I finally raised my teacup and replied,
"To all our days! The ones we've had and those yet to come!!"

He loved it. It was precious. And now, this has become our family's perfect toast!

CRANBERRY MORS DRINK

- 2 pounds fresh cranberries
- 3 1/2 Cups of sugar
- Orange zest
- Water
- Whole cloves to taste
- Passion or Raspberry tea
- Option: Dash of Vanilla Extract

1. Cover cranberries with water and boil for 10 minutes.
2. When cranberries come to a boil and pop, add in sugar and cook for 15 minutes on medium-low heat.
3. Add orange zest.
4. Optional: add in vanilla extract
5. Meanwhile, prepare at least a quart of your preferred tea and set aside.
6. Strain cranberries and put juice in a container and combine with tea. The consistency of this drink should be a heavier version of a hot tea.
7. Pour into cups

We drank this beautiful brew in a famous restaurant in St. Petersburg Russia. It is reminiscent of the aristocratic society, the days of Czars and the Nobles with their treasures of exquisite art and antiquities. It also calls us to the memory of common folk gathered around a wood burning fire, leathered, wrinkled skin, sparkling eyes full of laughter. Those who worked the land, grew the crops, raised chickens and cattle. Let us remember the goodness of those who have lived to make our lives better. Why not make a toast?

Here is our family toast; "To all our days, those we've had and those yet to come!"

I like to add a few cranberries and cloves into each cup that I serve. Our family and our friends will feel cherished and adored, they are after all, the royalty of our lives, so we should make them feel like it.

The Best Christmas Punch

-A Liles Family Tradition

- 2 small packages unsweetened raspberry koolaid
- 1 1/2 Cups sugar
- 3 quarts water
- 1 large can pineapple juice
- 1 6 oz can frozen lemonade, undiluted

1. Mix all ingredients in large container.
2. Serve over ice in pretty cups.

Lime Delish Drink

-By Janet Trout

- 8 limes
- 2 liters cold water
- 1 1/4 Cup sugar or to taste
- Optional: 1 lime sliced to garnish

1. Roll limes on the worktop or hard surface in a circular motion so they are easier to juice. You can also roll between your palms.
2. Cut and juice limes to make 1 cup of lime juice.
3. Add fresh lime juice in a pitcher with 2 liters of cold water, and stir.
4. Add in sugar.
5. Optional: add in sliced limes.
6. Serve, garnish and enjoy!

Snacks

"While you are in the world, you will have to suffer. But cheer up! I have defeated the world."

John 16:33

Crunch

- 2 Cups Cheerios
- 2 Cups Pretzels
- 2 Cups Wheat Chex
- 1 1/2 Cups Nuts
- 1/4 Cup Butter, melted
- 1/2 tsp Salt
- 1 tsp Worcestershire Sauce
- 1/2 tsp Celery Salt
- 1/2 tsp Garlic Salt

1. Combine all ingredients and make sure to thoroughly coat ingredients. Then put in a sealed container to keep fresh.

Cheese Puffs

- 4 ounces extra sharp cheddar cheese spread (room temperature)
- 1/2 Cup (1 stick butter, room temperature)
- 1 Cup all purpose flour
- Dash of paprika
- 3 jalapeños chopped (optional)

1. Preheat oven to 350 degrees.
2. Combine cheese and butter in medium size bowl and mix well.
3. Blend in flour.
4. Form into walnut size balls and place on a baking sheet.
5. Dust with paprika and refrigerate until thoroughly chilled.
6. Bake at 350 degrees until bottom of puffs are lightly browned, about 12-15 minutes.
7. Serve puffs hot out of the oven!

Chicken Wings

- 1 Cup white wine
- 1 1/2 Cup brown sugar
- 1/2 Cup Worcestershire Sauce
- 1/4 Cup butter
- 1/2 Cup water
- 1 Tbsp dry mustard
- 1 Tbsp ginger
- 16-18 chicken wings

1. Put butter and brown sugar in saucepan and warm until melted. Add remaining ingredients.
2. Add chicken wings to mixture, leave overnight in the fridge.
3. Line cookie sheet with foil and arrange wings on sheet.
4. Pour remaining juices over wings and bake at 350 degrees for 1 hour or until done.

Frito Pie

-By Priscilla McDonald McGruder, August 1978 Twin Falls, Idaho

- 1 small Bag Frito chips
- 1 pound grated Colby cheese
- 1 can Armour chili plain
- 1 can chili with beans and chili

1. Preheat oven to 350 degrees.
2. Heat both cans of chili together.
3. In 2 quart casserole dish, 1 layer of chips, 1 layer chili and repeat.
4. Top with cheese and bake at 350 degrees until cheese melts.

Broiled Cheese Puffs

- 1 baguette French bread loaf
- 5 Tbsp mayonnaise
- 1 Cup mild cheese, shredded
- 1 tsp Worcestershire Sauce
- 3 green onions, chopped

1. Turn on broiler
2. Mix all ingredients together to form a spread.
3. Toast one side of baguette.
4. Take each slice of baguette and put spread on the un-toasted side.
5. Arrange on a cookie sheet and put under broiler for 5 minutes or until it bubbles and is light brown.

Hot Wings by Meredith

- 24 Chicken wings
- Olive oil spray
- 1 Tbsp cayenne pepper
- 1 Tbsp chili pepper
- Paprika powder
- Garlic salt to taste
- Franks Hot Wing Sauce

1. Preheat oven to 415 degrees
2. Spray chicken wings with olive oil
3. Sprinkle wings with cayenne pepper, chili pepper, paprika powder and garlic salt.
4. Bake at 415 degrees on one side for 15 minutes and turn to bake for 10 minutes on the other side.
5. Then broil until wings are crispy.
6. Pour on the Franks Hot Wing Sauce! Voila!

This is a great snack during Uno games and Monopoly!

Spicy Hot Artichoke Dip

-This is a good way to get the kids to eat their vegetables.

- 3 cans of Artichoke hearts, not marinated, drained and cut into pieces
- 1 1/2 Cups mayonnaise
- 1 Cup grated Swiss cheese
- 1/4 Cup grated Parmesan cheese
- One clove of garlic peeled and chopped

1. Preheat oven to 350 degrees.
2. In a bowl, combine all ingredients.
3. Pour into a serving dish.
4. Bake 25 minutes until bubbling.
5. Keep warm when serving.
6. Serve with your favorite crackers, chips or crusty French Bread.

Hot Momma's Jalapeño Peppers

- 8 oz. whipped cream cheese
- 5 oz. Jalapeño Artichoke dip (Trader Joe's or Costco)
- 8 oz. sharp cheddar cheese grated (Separated in half)
- 6 oz. pepper jack grated (Separated in half)
- 1 pound bacon cooked and crumbled
- 12-15 Jalapeños

1. Preheat oven to 400 degrees.
2. Clean jalapeños and cut in half lengthwise. Remove seeds and then set aside.
3. In a bowl, combine cream cheese, Jalapeño artichoke dip, 4 oz sharp cheddar and 3 oz. pepper jack cheese.
4. Fill Jalapeño halves with cream cheese mixture.
5. Mix remaining cheddar and jack cheese together and sprinkle the tops of the filled peppers.
6. Place on baking sheet and sprinkle bacon on top.
7. Bake at 400 degrees until browned and bubbly! Approximately 15 minutes.

This is a "Storm of Delish!" Thank you to
Michelle Oliver who is the
Best Chef on the Central Coast!
Michelle made pans of these for our 50th
wedding anniversary party, they were a
smashing success! I make them often and there
is never one left over.

Hot Mama's Jalapeño Peppers

Pizza—RMG2's Mothers Recipe

-This is what she made and served for our rehearsal dinner on December 19, 1969, it was a hit!

Sauce:
- Large can tomatoes
- Salt & Pepper
- 1/3 Cup minced onion

Crust:
- Pillsbury hot roll mix, 1 box
- 1 Cup warm water

Cheese & toppings:
- Mild cheddar and mozzarella, grated
- Sausage and anything else desired

1. Preheat oven to 400 degrees.
2. Put large can of tomatoes into a blender to liquify, then put in large skillet.
3. Add salt, pepper and minced onion (can also add other Italian seasonings if desired).
4. Cook over medium heat until it cooks down to a paste. Stir often.
5. Use pillsbury hot roll mix and 1 cup of warm water. Grease a pan (I use a cookie sheet) and spread sauce over unbaked crust.
6. Place **grated mild cheddar and mozzarella on top.**
7. For **toppings, add sausage and anything else** desired. **Bake at 400 degrees until crust is light brown.**

Hot Cheddar Bean Dip

-It will melt your socks off!

- 1/2 Cup mayonnaise
- 16 ounce can of pinto beans (drained and slightly mashed)
- 1 Cup shredded cheddar cheese
- 4 ounces green chilies chopped
- 1/4 tsp hot pepper sauce (I prefer Tabasco)

1. Preheat oven to 350 degrees.
2. Combine all ingredients, pour into pan and bake at 350 degrees for 30 minutes.

Note: **cool slightly,** a lot of oil will surface, blot with **paper towel to remove** extra oil before serving. **Serve with chips of your** choice.

Apocalyptic Queso Cheese Dip

-My very favorite!

- 1 can (10 ounce) Rotel
- 1 (16 ounce) package Velveeta, cut into 1/2-inch cubes

1. Combine Rotel (do not drain) and Velveeta cheese in a medium saucepan.
2. Cook over medium heat until Velveeta is completely melted and mixture is well blended.
3. Stir frequently for 5 minutes, be careful to stir from the bottom so it doesn't stick and burn.
4. Serve warm with tortilla chips.

Someone told me that velveeta has a shelf life of 25 years or more?
All things considered it might be a good idea to keep a stash of velveeta in your cellar just in case of the Apocalypse.

Sweet & Savory Sauces, Dressings & Gravy

"Whenever two or three of you come together in my name, I am there with you".

Matthew 18:20

Lemon Butter Sauce

- 2 Shallots, diced
- 1 Cup White Wine
- 1 Ounce Champagne Vinegar
- 2 Ounces Heavy Cream
- 6 Ounces Sweet Butter
- Juice of One Lemon
- Salt and Pepper
- 1 Tbsp Chives

1. Combine shallots, wine and vinegar in a sauce pan.
2. Bring to a simmer and reduce by one half.
3. Add the heavy cream and reduce again.
4. Over low heat, whisk in the sweet butter piece by piece.
5. Season with salt and pepper and lemon juice.
6. Add the chives just before serving.

This sauce can be served with the Baby Pumpkin dish. It is quite delectable and can be used in conjunction with other recipes. Use your brilliant, creative, genius mind and come up with something outrageously good! Yes! You!

Louisiana Steak Sauce

- 1 stick butter
- 1/3 Cup Barbecue Sauce
- 2/3 Cup A-1 Sauce
- 2/3 Cup Worcestershire
- 2/3 Cup Heinz 57 Sauce
- 3/4 Cup Brown Sugar
- 1/3 Cup Ketchup

1. Cook all ingredients for a few minutes.
2. Serve warm with favorite cut of beef.

Bec Bec's Barbecue Sauce

-Cousin Becky is one of the very best cooks and bakers ever! Anything she makes is always THE BEST!

- 1 medium onion peeled and chopped
- 1 stick butter
- 4 cloves peeled chopped garlic
- 1 Cup molasses
- 1 Cup ketchup
- 1 Cup brown sugar (firmly packed)
- 2 Tbsp mustard
- 1 Tbsp Worcestershire sauce
- Ribs or chicken

1. Cook onions in melted butter and add garlic.
2. Cook until onions are clear.
3. Add ketchup, brown sugar, molasses, mustard and Worcestershire sauce.
4. Pre-cook beef or partially cook chicken.
5. Dip beef or chicken into sauce (complete emersion) place on cookie sheet and cook at 350 degrees for 45 minutes to one hour. Bake until tender.
6. Make sure you cook until the sauce "sets up" and thickens.

Best Caesar Dressing

-Awarded best of the best! My Mindy is a COOK! This girl of mine can whip up one seriously delicious salad in 5 minutes!

- 1/2 Cup olive oil
- 4 Tbsp mayonnaise
- 3 minced chopped garlic cloves
- 1/4 Cup Parmigiano Reggiano (parmesan shredded cheese)
- 2 Tbsp lemon juice
- 2 tsp white Worcestershire sauce

1. Mix all ingredients together.
2. Shake well before serving.

I use Romaine lettuce leaves to make up this salad. Enjoy!

Blue Cheese Dressing

- 3/4 Cup crumbled blue cheese
- 1/2 Cup sour cream
- 1/2 Cup buttermilk
- 1 small garlic clove
- 1 Tbsp white wine vinegar
- 2-3 dashes Worcestershire sauce or hot sauce
- 1 Tbsp chopped parsley
- Salt & Pepper to taste

1. Puree 1/2 cup each crumbled blue cheese and sour cream, 1/2 cup buttermilk, 1 small garlic clove (smashed) and 1 Tbsp white wine vinegar in a blender.
2. Transfer to a bowl and stir in 1/4 cup more blue cheese, 2-3 dashes of Worcestershire sauce or hot sauce, 1 Tbsp chopped parsley.
3. Season with salt & pepper.

Designer Salad Dressing

-December 31, 1999 Millennium Madness Spinach Salad saved the day!

- 1/2 Cup rice vinegar
- 1 Cup olive oil
- 4 cloves peeled, crushed garlic
- Pinch of kosher salt
- 1 Cup sugar
- Bunch of green onions cleaned and chopped
- 1 Cup feta cheese
- Washed and prepared spinach

1. In a jar with a lid, combine first 5 ingredients.
2. Shake it and shake again.
3. Place spinach in bowl, sprinkle green onions and feta cheese on top.

Thousand Island Dressing

- 1 Cup mayonnaise
- 3 Tbsp ketchup
- Dash of Worcestershire
- 1/4 Cup olives
- 1 boiled egg, diced
- Dash garlic salt

1. Mix all ingredients together.

Easy & Quick Spaghetti Sauce

- 3 pounds ground sirloin
- salt and pepper to taste
- 1 medium chopped onion
- 1 Tbsp garlic salt
- 2 Packages McCormick Spaghetti Mix with Mushrooms (dry mix)
- 1 large jar of vodka pasta sauce
- 1 Cup of pitted sliced olives
- 2 links sliced pepperoni
- Add water as needed

1. Brown the ground beef and salt and pepper to taste.
2. Add in chopped onions and a dash of garlic salt.
3. Add in McCormick spaghetti mix with mushrooms.
4. Add one large jar of vodka pasta sauce (or your preference) olives, pepperoni and water as needed.
5. Simmer sauce on low heat for 1-2 hours, stirring often from the bottom of the pot to keep sauce from sticking.
6. Makes approximately 2 quarts of sauce.

Pesto Sauce

-By The Randazzo Family (Al Leemans' Aunt Rickie's Recipe)

- 1 Cup Italian flat leaf parsley
- 2 Cups basil leaves (packed in)
- 1/2 Cup olive oil
- 6 large peeled garlic cloves
- 1/2 Cup grated Parmesan cheese
- 1/2 Cup melted butter

1. Put all ingredients into food processor and mix well.
2. Put into 1 quart ziplock bags.
3. Put in freezer immediately so it won't turn dark (lay flat in freezer).
4. Use for Pasta sauce.

Mother Leeman's Pasta Sauce

- 3-6 pounds 9 ounce cans Al Dente Pasta Sauce (from restaurant depot)
- 3- 14 ounce cans chopped tomatoes
- 2 large or 3 medium size white onions chopped
- 1/3 Cup chopped garlic cloves
- 1 pound chopped or sliced mushrooms
- 2 pounds mild Italian sausage (remove casings)
- 1 pound ground turkey
- 2 pounds ground beef
- 3 Cups White wine
- 1/2 Cup chopped basil
- 1/2 Cup chopped Italian parsley
- 2 Tbsp chopped rosemary
- 2 Tbsp chopped thyme
- 2 Tbsp dried oregano

1. Add pasta sauce and chopped tomatoes to a large pot.
2. Saute' white onions and garlic cloves then add them to the sauce.
3. Saute' sliced mushrooms and add to the sauce.
4. Saute' and deglaze pan with white wine. Add in Italian sausage, ground turkey and ground beef. Add more white wine (about 3 cups all together). Season meat with salt and pepper to taste as you saute'.
5. Add in all fresh herbs, finely chopped, to the sauce.
6. Cook sauce on low heat, stir often for 2-3 hours. Then 1 hour before it's done, taste and season if necessary.

Note: Mother Leeman likes to add in 3 tablespoons of white sugar at this time, but don't tell her son Duncan! What he doesn't know won't hurt him.

This is the most delicious pasta sauce! The Leeman family cooked the entire wedding dinner for our son Richard and our sweet daughter-in-love Meredith as a wedding gift. Dad Leeman and Duncan his son cooked this pasta sauce all day and served at least 200 people for that great celebration night. These are the rarest and dearest people, the very best, and have left their legacy of kindness, generosity and hospitality to bless countless others.

Moms Vanilla Sauce

- 1 cube butter
- 3/4 Cup sugar
- 1/4 Cup whipping cream
- 1 Tbsp vanilla

1. Melt butter in a pan.
2. Add sugar and cream.
3. When ingredients are smooth and golden, add vanilla and stir.

Note: This vanilla sauce can be served on or with just about any kind of dessert. It is diverse and irresistible!

Chocolate Sauce Topping

-Lilly's girl, Nancy Elliot Leonard

- 1 Cup evaporated milk
- 3 unsweetened baking chocolate squares
- 2 Cups sugar
- 1 tsp vanilla

1. Add ingredients to a sauce pan and boil for 5 minutes.
2. Add 1 teaspoon vanilla and beat with a mixer for 1 minute.
3. Serve.

Mom's vanilla
Sauce

The Gravy

-Awarded best of the best!

- 2-3 Tbsp butter
- 2-3 Tbsp flour
- 2 Cups chicken bouillon/broth
- 1/2 Cup of milk
- Drippings from turkey or beef
- 1/2 Cup sour cream
- Salt & Pepper

1. Melt butter in a pan, then add flour. Mixture should be cooked like a Roux.
2. Stay with it and continue to stir. This takes a few minutes so be patient! It should take on a deep brown hue and a nutty fragrance.
3. On medium heat, add into roux, chicken bouillon/broth. Stir in slowly then add 1/2 cup of milk.
4. Add drippings from turkey or roast beef, stir, then carefully add sour cream. Use a whisk to stir from the bottom of pan to keep gravy from sticking.
5. Salt and pepper to taste.

WARNING! This gravy is highly addictive and filled with unforgettable flavors! If you don't believe me, ask my children.

Kristopher's Secret Marinade Mix

- My girl Kate's husband and favorite human on the Earth.

- 1/2 Cup Rosemary
- 6 large cloves Garlic
- 1/4 Cup Thyme
- 1 tsp Chili flakes
- 1 tsp Smoked paprika
- 1/3 Cup Olive oil
- 1/3 Cup Red wine
- 2 Tbsp Kosher salt
- 1 tsp Kitchen Crack
- Lime zest
- 2 tsp Lime juice

1. In a bowl, mix and combine all ingredients and then puree'.
2. To use, cover meat with marinade, then wrap in foil and leave overnight in the refrigerator.
3. Take the meat out of refrigerator and let it warm to room temp before cooking.

Note: I normally start my lamb/meat on highest temp for 10 minutes then turn heat down and cook in a slow oven 325 degrees until desired doneness.

St. Jean & The Crow

My mother, "St. Jean," was the one to find the black crow hobbling on one tiny leg. Something had disabled this little creature, and it was near death when she discovered it among the wild woods and bushes lining the border of her beautiful private sanctuary.

In those early years, only a rugged, white-painted fence separated St. Jean's property from the hundreds of acres of gentle fields and small, tenacious streams springing up from God's pure delight. We played in those fields and swamps and streams, many days long after the sun was put to bed and had left just a few strands of its lingering beams to show us the way back home.

Ah, if only we could have captured and framed the timelessness of those carefree days. I worry that the children of today will never know or even want to see the mystery and breathless wonder of turning over a rock to find roly-poly bugs and wiggly worms and filling up jars of half pollywogs and half frogs in the making. It is worth a moment of our time to help the children of this world capture these critically important events, especially before they go on to the task of ruling and reigning and being stressed and worn by the journey of learning about living and dying.

I will never forget that dreadful day when, without any warning, the black and white jersey cows disappeared. Nobody seemed to know exactly who took them away or where they had gone. It was a sad day for all of us. We would no longer be able to stand along the fence and feed those cows who were like honorary family members and feel their noses nuzzling our hands. That was the moment Mother decided she would not lose her privacy to the invasion of a new subdivision bringing its towering two-story monster houses, loud neighbors hosting barbecues with blaring rock music, and other uncivilized goings-on.

Change is never easy, not for any of us, but especially for those who have nurtured, loved, and preserved the precious things we have long treasured and humbly relish the rewards that come from a lifetime of labor. Mother decided she would not give up her peaceful, gentle gardens of roses, lilies, hollyhocks, foxgloves (and who knows what else grew there) with volunteer seedlings sprouting up for the sheer gladness of Mother's smile! So, she set to work planting a 100-foot-wide by 25-foot-tall hedge of every kind of tree, bush, and bramble imaginable. This is where her crow convention and following began to spring up.

They (the crows) knew her as the Holy Scrap Lady, for as she threw out remnants from Sunday's dinner, days-old soured and surly leftovers, she quoted her favorite scriptures or even shouted the Jewish Shema:

"Sh'ma Yisra'eil, Adonai Eloheinu, Adonai echad!"
(Hear O Israel, the Lord is our God, the Lord is One!)

That's why she was called St. Jean by all of us who loved and knew her. She was a saint, and I am most confidently assured that even God and all of His angels agree!

Mother's crows were not just ordinary crows. If crows had souls, I am pretty sure they could easily be persuaded to apply for the fiery power of the same spirit that came from the heart of their guardian and feeder. They came from everywhere as Mother began her midday care and feeding of the community of homeless crows. This is where our story commences.

Mother saw the little black crow trying to get to the scraps of food, but the bigger, stronger crows would not allow it near their stockpile. Mother realized the predicament of this poor little guy and realized how close he was to giving up. She put on a pair of gloves, carefully gathered the weak, injured bird into her hands, and placed it in a cage that she had thoughtfully prepared with soft hay and wood shavings. She put food and water inside the cage, stroked the top of the little crow's head, then shut the door, making sure the lock was secured so the bird would rest and be safe through the night. For several weeks, this was her nightly ritual.

The little crow slowly became stronger, then one day Mother saw it try to stretch its wings and fly. When she thought it was finally ready to return to the big world, she left the door open, and it flew right out and headed straight into the forest of bushes and trees where it had first appeared. The little black crow sat on a tree branch looking at Mother as if to say, "Thank you for your help. I am all good now!"

That evening as shades of night began to appear; Mother went to her back porch to see if she might spot the improved little black crow. Much to her surprise and sheer joy, "Blackie", as Mother called him, had flown straight back into the cage, and after enjoying some seeds and a cool drink of water, happily nestled down for a good night's sleep.

This was such a fantastic story for Mother to tell, and no doubt the little black crow at long last had something astounding to crow about too! And crow he did! His voice was almost as loud and strong as all the other crows in the crow community, but none of them could brag about having their own bed and breakfast like Blackie!

Now, the exciting thing was that nobody seemed to notice that Blackie walked with a limp, or that his landings were less than perfect, or that he would often take a tumble head over tail. Nevertheless, Blackie had come into his own, and every crow in the community knew that he had "crowing rights"! Who else among all the crows in the entire Sonoma County could say that they had their own St. Jean to watch over them?

You see, I believe that God cares even about little broken birds. And if He cares about them, He must care a whole lot about every one of us who hurt and cry and carry around broken hearts. He sees, and He knows our need, and in His faithful love, we have His promise that He will never leave us or forsake us. God will send a St. Jean to see about us, to bring a tender touch, to pour the oil of hope, a healing balm into our wounds, to recite the blessing of the Shema, and to declare restoration upon our brokenness until we regain our strength and learn to walk again.

Special Thanks

I am so grateful for every person that contributed to the making of this book.

It is much more than a collection of recipes. It is a chronicle of glorious gatherings and beautiful smiling faces. It is the recollections of family gatherings and friends who have become family, sharing the blessing of wonderful food and good company.

A special thank you to every person who shared a favorite recipe. It is important that we hand down the timeless treasures of family recipes, so keep sharing!

I bless the memory of my mother and her mother, who both instilled a deep passion for cooking, baking and serving in my heart. They are the inspiration for this endeavor and I owe them so much. My hope is that my children and my grandchildren will embrace the priceless legacy of loving others through the gift of hospitality and good food.

To Jason West, Leah West and Monica Cabrillo, thank you for cheering me on.

Special Thanks

To Danae Dost, for your brilliance and organizational skills. You are amazing.

To my friend, Randa Chance, for your pristine editing and keeping me on track.

To my grandson, Josiah Gomes, for your creative photography genius that captured the smell and taste of my recipes.

To my niece, Nora Jorgensen, for the beautiful sketches that bring life to these stories. You are absolutely marvelous.

Jay C Winter Photography

Special thanks to Dawn Elizabeth Raney for proofreading and additional editing.

To Richard M. My love, my best friend, my husband of 52 years. You were the one who insisted on this recipe book. You make me believe that the offerings of my life are worthwhile and important. Thank you for your faith in me.

If there be any praise or glory for this recipe book let it be to our faithful God and Father from whom every blessing flows.

NG